BUDGET
MAKEOVERS

BUDGET MAKEOVERS

GIVE YOUR HOME A NEW LOOK

EDITED BY JEAN NAYAR

Woman's Day Specials   filipacchi
publishing

CONTENTS

INTRODUCTION

Creating a beautiful room doesn't require spending a fortune—as the spaces in this book readily prove. Some of the stunning makeovers featured on the pages that follow were pulled off for as little as $500 and involved hardly more than rearranging existing furnishings and accessories and applying a fresh coat of paint and some budget-savvy ingenuity. Others relied on higher limited budgets, but involved starting from scratch with all-new price-wise furniture or building on a bare-bones base with home-sewn slipcovers and window treatments or do-it-yourself headboards, picture frames and built-ins.

If you're ready to tackle your own cost-conscious makeover, the rooms in this book are sure to provide all the inspiration and know-how you'll need. Whether you want to refresh your family room, living room or dining room, or transform your kitchen, bedroom or bath, the wallet-friendly decorating ideas presented in these low-cost room redos will stimulate your imagination. Plus, easy-to-follow instructions for everything from shaped valances and bordered draperies to painted fire screens and built-in storage units will help you create customized decorative elements for your own rooms—at a price you'll love.

MAKEOVERS
ROOM
BY ROOM

CASUAL COMFORT

Ann Pederson loved the bones of her new suburban Virginia home, which she shares with her husband, Kirk, and their 4-year-old son, Ian. But because she favors a weathered lived-in look, she opted to warm up the family room, which doubles as an office for her home-based business, with a combination of flea-market finds, bargain shopping, some clever fabric ideas, and a little bit of paint.

The ambience in this room actually supports the work she does by serving as a marketing tool for her company, Posh Rooms, a successful home styling and decorating business. Her approach is budget-friendly, livable and fast. "I usually turn a room around in two weeks," says Ann, "and I decorate other homes with freshened flea-market pieces and clean backgrounds as I do in my own home."

In this room she painted the walls pale yellow and added generous touches of black with accessories and fabrics. She topped the sofa and ottoman with washable white slipcovers—for quick cleanups, she simply sprays them with a bleach mixture before washing. And she painted most of the furniture white or black.

To make the ceiling appear higher, Ann cut wallpaper remnants into 2-inch squares, then pasted the pieces onto the ceiling to make an attractive border. And she fashioned the draperies from tablecloths in a simple check pattern in rich colors, and then added a fringed trim to give them a custom look.

BEFORE

OPPOSITE: The family room showcases Ann Pederson's bargains. She covered cushions with toile and fabrics seen in adjoining rooms. The chairs are flea-market finds. Above the fireplace, Ann framed a tin ceiling tile with barn wood *(see p. 102 for instructions)*. The sisal rug picks up the checkered pattern in the draperies made from woven tablecloths.

ABOVE: On top of the pine armoire is a vintage breadmaker's sign. "It's a joke in our family, since I can't cook," says Ann. The white bookshelves are the first items Ann ever bought; baskets are used to store toys. Currently, Ann is eyeing the few unpainted surfaces left in her home. The pine armoire may get a coat of white paint—maybe the maple floors, too. *(See p. 102 for instructions for the ceiling border.)*

TIMELINE

- Planning . . . . **5 hours**
- Shopping . . . . **8 hours**
- Framing tile. . . . . **3 hours**
- Cutting and applying wallpaper diamonds . . . . **6 hours**
- Painting room . . . . **8 hours**
- Making tablecloth, drapes, pillows. **20 hours**

THE TAB

2 gallons of paint	$50.00
Wallpaper	50.00
Tin ceiling tile and materials	125.00
Bookshelves	50.00
Black-and-white checked rug (clearance)	10.00
Tablecloth (fabric and labor)	450.00
Draperies and pillows (fabric and labor)	500.00
Old sign	150.00
Armoire	500.00
TOTAL	**$1,885.00**

What They Loved

- The French doors are a great design feature.
- The armoire is big enough to hide the television.
- The fireplace as focal point.
- The gorgeous hardwood floors.
- The room opens onto the kitchen.

What They Hated

- The French doors are difficult to decorate around, because they limit the furniture arrangement.
- The room is a bit narrow; she'd prefer to have the sofas flanking the fireplace.
- The scale of the armoire. Eventually they want to replace it with a flat-screen TV and a painting to hide it.
- The room's dimensions, which make a symmetrical furniture arrangement impossible.

LEFT: In the family room, comfortable chairs invite family and clients—Ann's home office is in the armoire—to relax. The mirror at right was installed in an old door frame. Ann distressed and painted the desk, which she uses for writing personal correspondence. The $5 flea-market chair has a quilted slipcover.

UP CLOSE & PERSONAL

What kinds of things inspire you? I find ideas in hotels and shops wherever I travel.

How do tastes of family members influence your decor? My husband and son just want everything functional and comfortable—that means washable.

What are some of your favorite ways to keep things stimulating? Because there's a continuity of color throughout, I can switch objects and change vignettes from room to room whenever I want to.

How does your background influence your style? I grew up watching my mother decorate, so it was natural for me.

What six items can't you live without? I'd say our white slipcovers, natural elements like twigs and plants, candles and artwork. I also love the framed ceiling tile and mirror in the door frame—I appreciate their architecture.

What are your pet peeves? Dirt and clutter—every basket and cube can be used to store something.

Where do you find most of your bargain items? Flea markets. When I shop for clients, I look for myself, too.

What's one tip you can share about working with color? With a neutral background, changing accent colors can create a whole new look.

PRETTY AND PRACTICAL

OPPOSITE: The family room, or keeping room as Jane likes to call it, with its cushy slipcovered furniture and a rustic, oversize coffee table, is a cozy spot to gather. An antique rocking chair has a pillow in the window's check fabric. An old piano stool adds to the room's inviting simplicity.

When Jane Peterson and her husband, Greg, first decorated their house in Bardstown, Kentucky, they did it "very traditionally," she says. But after seven years, Jane was ready for a change. Armed with $60 worth of paint, she traded in the dull sage walls of the kitchen and the family room—which Jane refers to as the "keeping room," a Colonial-era term—for a cheery apple-green that is so bright, she jokingly advises visitors to put on sunglasses.

With two growing sons—Christopher, 14, and Andrew, 10—Jane wanted a more livable design scheme. She says she didn't want "dressy rooms you can't go into or enjoy."

Opting for a modern take on the French Country style, she created a vibrant color scheme for this room and the adjoining breakfast room and kitchen, pairing apple-green with black-and-white. When it came to furniture, Jane admits to using "a little of this and a little of that," mixing new furnishings with antiques that have been in the family for years, including an old rocker and a piano stool that serves as a side table.

The couple was able to add many clever decorative touches. "We're pretty handy," Jane says. "He does the woodwork part and I do the fabric part." So while Greg gave the older furnishings a new lease on life, Jane made the primary decorative statement with black-and-white toile Roman balloon shades, a design she created herself. To give the room a

What They Loved
- The room's gorgeous fireplace, which serves as its focal point, and the vaulted ceiling, which makes the room feel spacious.
- The windows, which provide a view out onto the woods nearby.
- The room's connection to the kitchen and breakfast area, which makes it all very family-friendly.

What They Hated
- The dreary dark sage color that brought down the friendly mood and didn't enhance the room's proportions or view.
- The lack of window treatments.
- The drabness of the space. A frequently used room like this should have a more fun feel.

THE TAB

Slipcovers	$250.00
Apple-green paint and supplies	60.00
Window treatment fabric	150.00
Fringe for lampshades	10.00
TOTAL	**$470.00**

OPPOSITE: The toile fabric turns up in the keeping room as balloon Roman shades, while check fabric is used for inverted pleats set off by black cording (see p. 103 for instructions). Black eyelash fringe was added to store-bought white silk lampshades (see p. 103 for instructions).

TIMELINE
- Planning . . . . **4 hours**
- Shopping . . . . **4 hours**
- Painting . . . . **5 hours**
- Making window treatments . . . . **10 hours**
- Applying fringe to lampshades . . . . **½ hour**

unified look without buying new furniture, she covered a sofa and chair with crisp, easy-care white slipcovers. Then she crafted an assortment of finishing touches: accent pillows made from the same black-and-white toile and complemented with checks and trims; lampshades covered with toile and enhanced with whimsical eyelash fringe. The end result is a cozy, colorful and perfectly primed space for family living.

DO'S AND DON'TS FOR CREATING FAMILY-FRIENDLY ROOMS

Do add architectural interest. Simple inexpensive crown molding installed around the perimeter of a ho-hum room injects instant character.

Don't paint walls a stark, sterile white. If you must go with white, select a shade that has some pigment in it, like Linen White or Antique White. But, colored walls with white trim are an unbeatable combination.

Do choose forgiving fabrics like cotton, denim, linen or chenille. For an all-around neater look, pick easy-care slipcovers in a tailored shape.

Don't purchase a set of matching furniture. Incorporating antiques or vintage pieces that you love with new pieces will give the room a unique personal style.

Do buy the most comfortable upholstered furniture you can afford with deep seats for lounging and well-padded arms to withstand daily wear.

Don't show off the TV. Find a cabinet—one you paint yourself would be fabulous—for the TV to keep it out of sight during special family times.

FAMILY FRIENDLY

BEFORE

ABOVE: Bare windows at the opposite end made the room look cold and let in too much damaging sunlight.

OPPOSITE: London shades, topped with a valance, bring a softly tailored counterpoint to the spare wood blinds, which now cover all windows in the room.

What They Loved
- The cozy fireplace.
- The vaulted ceiling.
- The built-in bookshelves, woodwork, and window seat.

What They Hated
- The messiness.
- The unfinished look of the window frames and window seat.
- The lack of window treatments.

When Susan and Andy Carpenter moved from a Manhattan brownstone to a sprawling, 100-year-old Colonial home in Somerset County, New Jersey, one of their favorite aspects of the place was its site. "We overlook an enormous rolling meadow that makes us feel like we're in a rural area instead of a suburb," says Susan. Little did she know the remarkable vista would become a sticking point for her husband when she began discussing the prospect of creating the window treatments she'd been dreaming of.

The couple had only basic shades in their last place, because "we thought anything else wouldn't work well with the contemporary art and graphic Turkish rugs we collect," Susan explains. But in their new house, "the rooms are huge, much more formal—and the light is almost too bright. We needed something to soften them up," she says. "But Andy loved to be able to look outside at the view," she adds. As an art director for a large publishing group, he also had an informed aesthetic on color and style. "He didn't want the house to be too feminine, since both our children are girls, and he didn't want anything to clash with the rugs," she notes.

Fortunately, Susan, who is a marketing consultant for museums, has a similar point of view. But she was certain that the window treatments would be a good addition to the house since they would help control the light and glare and make the rooms

TIMELINE

- Measuring windows . . . . **1 hour**
- Reviewing design options . . . . **1 hour**
- Ordering, reviewing and choosing fabrics and trims . . . . **2½ hours**
- Window treatment fabrication, plus shipping time . . . . . . **40-hour week**
- Painting window molding . . . . **4 hours**
- Purchasing, cutting, applying and painting molding
  to window seat . . . . **4 hours**
- Ordering blinds, window treatments and pillows . . . . **1 hour**
- Installing blinds and shades . . . . **6 hours**
- Adding pillows, hanging artwork, switching out accessories . . . **½ hour**

ABOVE: With a blind on only one window, unpainted window molding and a cushionless window seat, the space looked unfinished.

OPPOSITE: A layered window treatment along with a few new cushions provide warmth at the window seat.

look more finished and intimate. For her family room, Susan had gathered ideas from decorating publications and catalogs and collected her thoughts on color—she was drawn to bright primaries, which she felt would set off the family's contemporary art. In this setting, simple, striped Roman shades topped with a self-valance add just the right touch of warmth without excessive formality. For extra practicality and polish, she opted to layer the shades over painted wooden blinds that allow her to adjust the light as needed throughout the day. Sue also added a bevy of cushions—edged with simple piping or fringe—to the window seat to make it more inviting.

Before the window treatments were installed, however, Andy, who enjoys carpentry in his spare time, painted the raw wooden window frames white to match the rest of the molding in the room and added new strips of molding to the window seat to give it a more finished built-in look.

THE TAB

4 shades with self-valance and mounting hardware	**$1,686.00**
4 wooden blinds with specialty tape and mounting hardware	647.00
2 pillows with cording	56.00
2 quarts of primer and paint	30.00
9 feet of molding	6.00
Nails	1.50
Picture hook	1.00
TOTAL	$2,427.50

ABOVE: London shades, topped with a valance *(see p. 104 for instructions)*, bring a softly tailored counterpoint to the spare wooden blinds, which now cover all windows in the room.

ISLAND RETREAT

Peter Walsh loved his parents' Shelter Island, New York, home so much that he bought it when they retired. "The deal was that they'd take the good stuff out and leave the rest," says Peter, an editor with Woman's Day Special Interest Publications. What remained at the 25-year-old Cape, which sits on a wooded acre, was a ragtag collection of furnishings, which he added to finds from flea markets and the local landfill.

Peter's color palette for the living/dining room—beeswax-colored walls and off-white trim—was neutral, warm and cozy. "But in summer," he says, "with leaves on the trees and not much light coming in, the room looked dark." Worse, it always felt cluttered and poorly organized. Enter a little help from his design editor friends, who knew they could cheer up the space with a few low-cost updates and simple changes. They began by touring the house and gathering some of Peter's accessories that they felt would enhance and unify the space.

Knowing that Peter's makeover budget was only $500, the editors mostly rearranged, reused or refurbished existing furniture and accent pieces, and made a few important purchases: slip-covers, pillows, throws and a lampshade, plus tools they needed for modest fix-ups. The ivory, bone, khaki and blue palette of their simple scheme so brightened the space that it feels like a completely different room.

BEFORE

ABOVE: The dining area was barren except for the farm table and rustic bench. An extra table floated nearby with no real purpose.

OPPOSITE: Peter cleaned an old doorless pie safe, then the designers filled it with choice ceramic pieces. Stick-on paper shades give the windows a crisp finish. The old floor lamp was painted to give it a new life *(see p. 105 for instructions).*

RIGHT: Peter relaxes on his newly slipcovered sofa, with plump pillows replacing the old back cushions. Some lattice was cut and stained to make a low-cost frame for the eastern Long Island map *(see pp. 105–106 for instructions)*, which ties in perfectly with the room's palette. It replaces an abstract painting that was moved upstairs.

BEFORE

What He Loved

- Space and spaciousness. The living room is about 240 square feet. Having living and dining in one big room with a fireplace has a homey feel.
- Light and view. Except in summer, the windows let in natural light, and there are views of the surrounding woods and the gardens he created.
- The shell of the room. The paint tones were Peter's choices. And, he says, "There is old-fashioned charm in the scuffed-up look of the original pine floor."
- The furnishings. The sofa had been his grandmother's; the farm table and benches belonged to his parents. "I found the coffee table at a yard sale," Peter recalls. "It's an old ship's hatch mounted on curving wrought-iron legs."
- The artwork. The designers hung a small oil landscape painting from the upstairs hall and a Shelter Island sign from the garage—pieces Peter didn't know what to do with—in the dining area.

What He Hated

- Mismatched furniture. The yellow slipcovered sofa and orange slipcovered club chairs were fine in scale, but their colors made the room feel dreary.
- Too little focus, too much rusticity. The corner where the chaise sat was cluttered and didn't tie in with the rest of the room. A poorly finished floor lamp topped with a faded amber shade had a nice shape but didn't relate to the decor either.
- The fireplace. The red brick seemed dated. "Someday I'll lighten the look with whitewash," says Peter.
- No cohesiveness. The new slipcovers, pillows and accents establish a seaside-inspired blue, tan and white color scheme and Shelter Island theme.

THE TAB

1 sofa slipcover	$150.00
2 chair slipcovers	118.00
1 lampshade	41.00
2 fringed pillows	30.00
2 striped pillows	22.00
1 denim pillow	20.00
4 window shades	19.88
1 chenille throw	16.99
16 feet of 2½-inch-wide lattice (to make frame)	16.00
1 piped pillow	15.00
1 tasseled pillow	12.99
2½ yards leather cording (to trim lampshade)	5.00
Wood stain (for frame)	4.99
Polyurethane (for frame)	4.99
Spray paint (to refurbish lamp)	4.98
1 finial	4.50
1 yard grosgrain ribbon (to trim floor lamp lampshade)	4.30
Porcelain ball	3.00
¾-inch brads (for frame)	1.29
TOTAL	**$494.91**

ABOVE: A footstool Peter once gave his mother sits in front of a slipcovered club chair. The sisal rug was among Peter's first acquisitions. The mirror, which helps to reflect light, the decorative bottle, the baskets and the sailboat model came from other rooms.

BEFORE

ACCENTUATE THE POSITIVE

Do use floor or table lamps in addition to ceiling fixtures. Their soft glow creates a cozier ambience than the harsh illumination and shadows cast by a single overhead fixture.

Don't shy away from large-scale accessories. Too many people play it safe by choosing lots of small items, which can just end up cluttering the space. A grandly scaled mirror or artwork draws the eye directly to the fireplace; large hurricane lamps act as punctuation marks for the mantel.

Do consider the scale of the room when choosing furniture. A large, overstuffed chair that might be tempting for its cushiness factor would look overpowering in this not-so-large living room.

Don't be afraid to layer area rugs over wall-to-wall carpeting. Rugs in a rich color or interesting pattern can emphasize seating areas or pathways from the living room to the kitchen or the foyer.

Do accentuate the height of tall windows by mounting drapery rods above the window and placing tiebacks for the draperies up high.

ABOVE: The lamp was found in the basement. Whipstitching leather cording through holes in the top of a new paper lampshade gives it color and texture (see p. 105 for instructions).

OPPOSITE: A new throw was hung on an old ladder found in the garage. The chaise cushion was re-covered with a remnant of fabric Peter had in his collection of flea-market textiles. The ceramic lamp, which came from Peter's bedroom, makes a strong focal point on the table. The framed map of Shelter Island in the 1950s—one of Peter's garage-sale finds—adds to the nautical theme the editors decided on to help unify the room.

TIMELINE

- Reviewing Peter's photos and discussing the possibilities . . . . **1 hour**
- Choosing and ordering slipcovers and pillows from catalogs . . . . **¾ hour**
- Touring Peter's house . . . . **2 hours**
- Bringing reusable objects from various parts of the house to the living/dining room . . . . **2 hours**
- Removing clutter and some furniture and accessories . . . . **1½ hours**
- Rearranging furniture, putting recycled pieces into place and applying slipcovers . . . . **2 hours**
- Making a list of new accessories and tools to buy and projects to undertake . . . . **1 hour**
- Shopping . . . . **8 hours**
- Cutting, staining and constructing the map frame, spray-painting the floor lamp, trimming the lampshades . . . . **3½ hours**
- Putting new and refurbished accessories in place . . . . **½ hour**

HAPPY HOME

BEFORE

ABOVE: An oak armoire—topped with old baskets and housing the television—once dominated the back wall in the family room. The mismatched seating was sparse and uncomfortable, even though Judy and Bob spend much leisure time here.

OPPOSITE: One of the Walshes' wicker chairs, sporting a newly covered seat cushion and new pillow *(see p. 106 for instructions)*, now resides in the redecorated living room. A huge framed mirror over a new sofa reflects natural light pouring in through the shuttered window, making the room feel more expansive. A glass-topped coffee table heightens the impact of the burgundy area rug.

The longer Judy and Bob Walsh lived in their new farmhouse-style home in Port Jefferson Station, New York, the more they knew that their decorating ideas weren't working. "We have a large extended family and love to entertain," Judy says, "but as we also have a big eat-in kitchen, we felt we really didn't need a dining room. What we did need was a family room, where each of us could read, listen to music or watch TV." So the couple turned their dining room into an improvised family room—with some old chairs and a television in an armoire—and spent most of their time there. But they rarely used the adjoining living room, which they closed off from the family room by placing a love seat and a sofa virtually back-to-back to block the extra-wide entrance to the space.

"Judy and Bob wanted a total makeover with new furnishings to make both spaces more inviting," says Jean Nayar, editor of Woman's Day Special Interest Publications' *Budget Decorating Ideas* magazine, who masterminded this room redo. "But they wanted to keep the cost under $3,000. Knowing of sources near the Walshes' home where I could find a full range of quality furnishings at the right prices, I visited the stores taking snapshots of furniture and accessories I felt Judy and Bob would like."

"It was Jean's idea to open up the two rooms and treat them as one continuous space," Judy recalls. Jean explains: "I felt by opening up the two spaces and linking them with complementary

ABOVE: A pair of new armchairs, upholstered in a soft burgundy chenille, warms up the living room and links it to the hues in the family room.

furniture and colors, they would read as one harmonious whole. I drew a floor plan so the Walshes could see how to orient the furniture they chose toward a logical focal point in each room and gain a sense of the flow between the rooms."

Comfort is the theme of the family room, and warmth—with furniture grouped around the fireplace—is key in the living room. New area rugs help define the seating areas and their different colors give each space its own identity. The rugs also set the stage for the colors in the rooms, which Jean calls "an all-American palette: burgundy, navy blue, khaki, and a bit of olive-green." The makeover began with the stark white walls. "I suggested a warm, ivory paint, and Bob did the work," says Jean. To keep within budget, she urged the Walshes to reuse a few existing pieces—the television armoire, a sofa table and two wicker chairs—and moved them into new spots within the updated arrangement. Floor-length draperies flanking the shuttered window provide a soft finishing touch in the living room. Delighted with the transformation, Judy says, "We never used to go in the living room—now we're in there all the time."

What They Loved
- The fact that the rooms opened onto each other, so neither room felt boxy or confined.
- The wood-burning fireplace in the living room. "It's now a focal point, a place people gather around when they visit us," says Judy.
- The abundance of light and the views.
- The piano. Music is important to the couple; their upright has long been in the family.

What They Hated
- The lack of cohesiveness. "Everything was mismatched," says Bob.
- The furniture in the family room. It was old and uncomfortable.
- The clumsy arrangement of furnishings.
- The coldness of both spaces. Bob calls the former wall color "builder's white—the look was not only cold but uninviting."

TIMELINE

The Walshes wanted a makeover done as quickly as possible.

- Reviewing the "before" shots and developing a rough scheme . . . . **2 hours**
- Visiting the furniture store and taking snapshots of furniture and accessories . . . . **½ day**
- Visiting the homeowners to show furniture photos and make selections . . . . **½ day**
- Scouting the Walsh home in search of reusable furnishings . . . . **½ day**
- Compiling a list of purchases and placing orders at the store . . . . **2 hours**
- Moving existing furnishings out of the homeowners' living and family rooms . . . . **½ day**
- Painting the walls in two rooms . . . . **1 day**
- Receiving furniture shipment and assembling furniture . . . . **½ day**
- Putting new furniture and existing pieces in place in both rooms . . . . **½ day**
- Shopping for ready-made curtains . . . . **2 hours**
- Searching for and buying appropriate curtain hardware . . . . **½ day**
- Cutting and painting dowel for use as curtain rod, and mounting curtain hardware . . . . **2 hours**
- Hanging artwork and mirror . . . . **1 hour**
- Ironing and hanging curtain panels . . . . **1 hour**
- Choosing fabrics and covering cushions . . . . **4 hours**

BEFORE

OPPOSITE: A cushy love seat on a blue rug splashed with floral accents was placed to face the fireplace, the living room's focal point. New ready-made linen panels frame the shuttered window on a rod Bob created himself from a 14-foot wooden dowel. The new wood-and-metal end tables and coffee table lend warmth and Asian-inspired accessories add a colorful exotic touch.

LEFT: The living room was once seen over the back of a love seat that completely blocked the large opening from the adjacent family room.

THE TAB

1 sofa	$499.00
1 love seat	449.00
2 burgundy upholstered armchairs	398.00
1 leather armchair	349.00
4 curtain panels	256.36
1 wood-and-metal cocktail and 2 side tables	149.00
1 glass-topped metal cocktail and 2 side tables	149.00
1 large framed mirror	99.00
2 area rugs	79.98
1 framed oil painting	59.99
3 yards of decorative fabric	57.00
2 brass torchère lamps	49.98
2 urn lamps	49.98
4 sets of curtain rings	39.96
1 wrought-iron bench	29.99
2 chenille throws	29.98
2 gallons of paint	13.98
2 burgundy woven pillows	13.98
1 quart of black high-gloss paint	13.00
2 metal finials	12.99
1 blue-and-black Chinese vase	9.99
1 large framed rooster print	9.99
1 blue-and-black covered bowl	7.99
2 white pillar candles	3.98
1 wooden dowel as curtain rod	2.99
TOTAL	**$2,834.11**

ABOVE: A comfy leatherette chair, soft throw and casual artwork create a relaxing reading corner in the family room. The piano bench in the living room beyond sports a new cover in a fabric that ties together the palette of the two rooms.

LEFT: A soothing palette and soft textures make the living room inviting.

COUNTRY CLASSIC

In the process of redecorating their dining room, Jane Peterson and her husband, Greg, undertook the project with the same spirit of teamwork they embraced while redecorating almost every other room in the home they share in Bardstown, Kentucky, with their two sons, Christopher and Andrew. As in the other rooms, Jane took on the sewing projects, while Greg handled the painting and repurposing existing pieces of furniture.

A sunny space with a large window and white wainscoting, the dining room used to function as an informal study for the family. But Jane and Greg decided they wanted an attractive space for entertaining and family gatherings; they restored the room to its original purpose with a mix of new accent pieces, antique furnishings and family heirlooms.

The couple wanted the space to look polished and pretty without being formal. So instead of covering the windows with a heavy window treatment, Jane opted for a simple pleated valance with jabots, which she crafted herself and trimmed with fringe. Cleverly rethinking the placement of other pieces in the house, Jane "hijacked" a bedroom dresser to serve as a foyer table leading into the dining room. She turned a kitchen island her husband had refinished and painted white into a dining room sideboard. The dining room's chairs, found in an aunt's attic, were in pieces; Greg reassembled and painted them, and

BEFORE

OPPOSITE: Formerly used as a study, complete with desk and computer, the new dining room is a mix of old and new, from antique mirrors to oak chairs, a tole tray to painted pottery. Prints bought in Paris share wall space with timeless silhouettes of Jane's relatives.

What They Loved
- The room's high ceilings, and its good size with nice proportions.
- The neutral color. It emphasized the natural light streaming in.

What They Hated
- The room's design; it was a hodgepodge.
- The fact that the room served as a makeshift home office with a computer area. The office equipment was visible even as you passed by the room.

Jane added seat cushions, which she made with leftover fabric from her own pleated valance. Greg also painted the sideboard, acquired at an unfinished-furniture shop.

A mix of charming accents, including a tole tray, brightly painted teapots, dollar prints from Paris custom framed and grouped to remind the family of their trip, and silhouettes of Jane's mother and aunt on wall-mounted pedestals, add more color and a decidedly personal air to the relaxed, inviting room.

TAB

White chairs (found in aunt's attic; husband reassembled)	**Free**
Wood chairs (4 at $25 each found at auction sale)	**$100.00**
Caning supplies for wood chairs	**40.00**
Fabric and supplies for window treatment	**70.00**
Mirror above sideboard (antique sale)	**20.00**
Sideboard (from unfinished-furniture store)	**600.00**
TOTAL	**$830.00**

ABOVE: A pair of pillows *(see p. 108 for instructions)* repeats the window treatment. The complementary plaid pillow has matching fringe and a row of accent buttons on the front.

DO'S & DON'TS FOR MIXING STYLES

Do consider the context. The architecture of your home, as much as individual likes and dislikes, will dictate which design styles will work.

Don't forget to do your homework. Look through magazines and rip out pages of furnishings or settings you like. Then talk about whether the two of you can live with them together.

Do work together. Embrace the unexpected. Unusual combinations can create an interesting, eclectic look.

Don't hesitate to express your feelings. Understand each other's temperament. Does he like a sophisticated, urban look? Does she prefer a look that's relaxed and laid-back? Think about how the environment can reflect both of you.

TIMELINE

- Planning. . . . . **5 hours**
- Shopping . . . . **8 hours**
- Stripping and finishing wood chairs . . . . **20 hours**
- Re-caning wood chairs . . . . **40 hours**
- Making window treatment . . . . **8 hours**
- Refinishing mirror above sideboard . . . . **4 hours**
- Sanding and painting sideboard . . . . **3 hours**

ABOVE: After deciding that swags were too formal, Jane dressed the window with a pleated valance with jabots *(see p. 107 for instructions)*. She used a rose-colored fabric and trimmed it with ivory fringe. Jane stores dishes, in shades of cream, yellow and green, in the butler's pantry. The polka-dot glasses are her "little touch of whimsy."

OPPOSITE: The wrought-iron chandelier and lamps were "real bargains," says Jane, who changes the shades seasonally. Greg repaired the mirror that Jane found at an auction.

FARMHOUSE FRESH

BEFORE

ABOVE: Bare windows and mismatched, multicolored chairs fell short of the formality of the dining room.

OPPOSITE Floor-length draperies topped with a scalloped valance *(see pp. 108–109 for instructions)* bring refreshing balance to the formal room. The polished look of the treatments inspired the wife to paint and recover her chairs with a quilted contrasting fabric *(see p. 110 for instructions)*.

One of the things Susan and Andy Carpenter cherish most about their 100-year-old Colonial home in Somerset County, New Jersey, is the view of the surrounding rolling meadow visible from almost every room in the house. The pastoral landscape is especially lovely through the massive bay window in their dining room. But without decorative treatments to frame this window, not only did the view seem to lose some of its impact but the room felt cold and bare—and lacked the sense of polish Susan craved for the space.

Since the couple frequently entertains, Susan wanted to give the room—which is quite large and rather formal—a sense of substance without being fussy. She and Andy enjoy collecting contemporary art that displays wit and strong color. So Susan wanted window treatments that would complement the cheery room's yellow walls without competing with the art. Jean Nayar, editor of Woman's Day Special Interest Publications' *Budget Decorating Ideas* magazine, helped her find fabrics that would work in the space—and after Susan chose a lovely tone-on-tone woven-vine pattern, Jean created a design for the window treatments in keeping with Susan's vision for the space. Fabricated by a friend, the floor–length draperies and pleated Queen Anne–inspired valance give the room an air of contemporary elegance while beautifully framing the window and adding a feeling of height to the

RIGHT: A flat braid gives a crisp finish to the scalloped pleated valance, which spans the width of the large bay window and adds a feeling of height and grandeur to the room.

What They Loved
- The ample size of the room.
- The big bay window overlooking a pastoral view.
- The lovely wood paneling.

What They Hated
- The dark quality of the room.
- The fact that the room was unfinished.
- The cold ambience due to the lack of window treatments.

TIMELINE

Measuring window and surrounding area . . . . ½ **hour**

Reviewing design ideas . . . . 1 **hour**

Designing window treatment . . . . 5 **hours**

Searching for and choosing fabric . . . . 4 **hours**

Calculating yardage, ordering fabric.. . . . . 1½ **hours**

Fabricating window treatment. . . . . 16 **hours**

Purchasing and cutting lumber. . . . . 1½ **hours**

Purchasing brackets, rods, and mounting hardware . . . . 1 **hour**

Constructing and mounting valance and hanging draperies . . . . . 3 **hours**

Repainting chairs . . . . 2 **hours**

Recovering chair seats . . . . 1 **hour**

space. The scalloped valance is also finished with a custom trim, which Susan desired. "Jean suggested trims that would work with these treatments and I really like the effect," she says. The fully lined window treatments not only add beauty to the room—but function, too. In spring and summer months, they help control the light that pours in through the generous windows; during the fall and winter they help keep the room warm by adding a layer of insulation over the windows.

After Susan and Jean mounted the valance and installed the panels, they tackled the furniture. Andy had fabricated a new dining table from recycled barn wood—but the casual mismatched chairs that surrounded were painted in several different colors and no longer worked in the space now that the window treatments gave it an ambience of easy elegance. So Susan painted all of the chairs black to match the table. Then she chose another lovely fabric—this one was red, with a woven pattern of yellow bumblebees—to recover the chairs. Jean and Susan simply cut pieces of the fabric to fit over the seats and used a staple gun to tack them on.

In keeping with her taste for vivid color, this room incorporates a palette of primaries—with yellow the dominant color on window treatments and walls, and secondary shades of red on the chairs and bold blue in the artworks. Finally, a new chunky crystal-like chandelier finishes off the room with a glittering touch of whimsy.

DO'S AND DON'TS FOR DINING SPACES

Do use ready-made frames with a mat. It's easy to slip kids' art into them and display it. Children feel good when their parents think their work is important enough to frame.

Don't be afraid if dining room furniture doesn't match. Painted chairs look great with a wood table that has a natural finish.

Do employ your dining room table for multiple functions—as a home office or study desk, for example.

Don't hang chandeliers close to the ceiling. The goal is to light the top of the table, about 30 to 36 inches above the surface, so diners can see what they're eating and there's still plenty of room for floral arrangements.

Do add lights to the interiors of wooden bookcases and cabinets. Any good frame shop or art gallery will have a selection of tiny lights that you can secure to the top or bottom of the cabinet's interior.

Don't rely on a single source of lighting. Either sconces and/or recessed cans in the corners of a room, all connected to dimmer switches, are perfect companions to a chandelier and allow you to create a variety of light moods.

TAB

10 yards of drapery fabric	$750.00
10 yards of lining	30.00
15 yards of trim	45.00
Thread and sewing sundries	10.00
Lumber	12.00
Brackets and curtain hardware	15.00
Spray paint	10.00
5 yards of chair fabric	250.00
Screws and butterfly nuts	2.00
TOTAL	**$1,124.00**

VICTORIAN BEAUTY

"I always wanted a dining room.

I never had one—I'd lived in apartments all my life," says Barbara Winfield, editor of Woman's Day Special Interest Publications' *Home Remodeling & Makeovers* magazine. So when she and her friend, artist Miriam Hernández, bought a 100-year-old Victorian in Jeffersonville, New York, her first thought was to make a switch. A smallish dining room became the living room, and the 12 x 17-foot living room—prime space at the front of the house—became the dining room. "We needed the extra space; we do a lot of entertaining," Barbara explains. To help make her dining room look fresher and more inviting, yet keep it in the spirit of the house, she turned to Jean Nayar, editor of Woman's Day Special Interest Publications' *Budget Decorating Ideas* magazine.

With Jean's help, Barbara's dining room became a beautiful setting for the furnishings, many of which were pieces she had collected over time. Barbara had already tackled the first steps in redoing the room—resurfacing and repainting its walls. (The previous owners had removed paneling and the dropped ceiling that had been applied in the 1970s to expose the original 10-foot-tall ceilings; and in the process, had left badly gouged plaster surfaces.) She also replaced the crown and base molding that had been removed and had the wood floors refinished.

To decorate the room, Barbara worked with Jean to develop a crisp, cool style inspired by Swedish design. Barbara and

BEFORE

ABOVE: Before the room was decorated, the windows were bare; a dingy, worn rug covered the floor; and industrial-looking metal chairs surrounded the table.

OPPOSITE: Original to the room, the ceiling medallion and elegant stained-ash woodwork were in serviceable condition when Barbara Winfield and Miriam Hernández moved in. They added the molding, and a friend created the chair-seat covers and window treatments. The shaped valances *(see pp. 110–111 for instructions)* with beaded trim were mounted 7 inches above the tops of the windows to emphasize the height of the space.

RIGHT: The wall mirror, which Barbara once gold-leafed, was hung higher than before to balance with the windows, which look taller topped with their new valances. Paper shades were brought in for the chandelier (see p. 112 for instructions)

What She Loved

- The shape and scale of the room, which is gracious enough for friends to linger in comfortably after a meal.
- The four tall windows, which present views to both the front and side of the house.
- An intact plaster ceiling medallion, original to the room.
- Dark-stained woodwork and Victorian trim. (A previous owner had protected them with an unsightly coating of shellac, which Barbara plans to remove.)

What She Hated

- The worn floors, which needed to be restored.
- Hideous green walls, which bore the scars and nail holes of paneling that had been removed.
- Bare windows, which made the room feel empty and cold.

OPPOSITE: Barbara uses a pie safe from the 1850s to store china. Jean topped it with some Chinese porcelain bowls and candlesticks from Barbara's collection. She then mounted a quartet of framed botanicals, which tie in with the colors and pattern of the chair-seat covers.

TIMELINE

Barbara's dining room is in her weekend home, so she could work on it only on Saturdays and Sundays. Here's how much time Barbara, Miriam and a few of their friends and colleagues spent on it:

- Plastering and painting walls. . . . . **Three weekends**
- Refinishing the floor. . . . . **Three 8-hour days**
- Cutting and installing crown molding . . . . **5 hours**
- Cutting and installing baseboards . . . . **12 hours**
- Sanding and painting dining table. . . . . **3 hours**
- Priming and painting chest . . . . **3 hours**
- Shopping for fabrics. . . . . **3 hours**
- Designing valances and chair-seat covers . . . . **8 hours**
- Sewing valances and chair covers . . . . **Four 8-hour days**
- Shopping for furniture and accessories . . . . **6 hours**
- Purchasing mounting boards and hardware. . . . . **2 hours**
- Installing valances . . . . **5 hours**
- Putting together chairs, adding seat covers . . . . **3 hours**
- Hanging artwork and rehanging mirrors . . . . **2 hours**

Miriam stripped and sanded the table—a found piece crudely covered with self-stick paper—then painted it white. Jean helped Barbara find pastel fabrics, affordable wooden chairs and an unfinished cabinet, which they painted pale yellow to pick up on a color in the new fabrics. Valances were a priority for Barbara. She wanted just enough of a treatment to dress up the windows without blocking the view. Jean designed the window treatments and chair-seat covers, added a bench and plant stand from other rooms, and brought in paper shades for the chandelier, a gift to Barbara from cousins, finishing them off with a touch of trim.

ABOVE: Jean designed the tie-on chair-seat covers (*see pp. 111–112 for instructions*) and suggested replacing a worn floor-covering with a simple sisal rug. The pretty, low-cost chairs came painted but unassembled; a coworker helped Barbara snap them together.

OPPOSITE: More storage was needed, so Jean urged Barbara to replace a trunk with an unfinished wooden chest, which, when painted, became the perfect place to store and display serving pieces. She rehung Barbara's antique mirrors above it in a symmetrical arrangement that relates to the height of the cabinet and shows off the lines of the mirrors to more dramatic effect.

RIGHT: Barbara's collection of antique mirrors had been mounted haphazardly above an old wooden trunk on one wall of the room.

THE TAB

Floor sanding, repairing and staining	$400.00
1 unpainted wood chest	315.00
6 white-painted wood chairs	239.94
Fabric for valances	237.93
1 sisal rug	229.00
Fabric for 6 seat covers	203.94
8 paper lampshades	132.92
4 framed floral prints	99.67
Brushes plus primer and paint for wood furniture	75.00
Bead trim for valances	47.84
Nails, screws, mounting boards, picture hooks	38.01
Rollers plus wall and ceiling primer and paint	25.06
Grosgrain ribbon to trim lampshades	4.41
TOTAL	**$2,048.72**

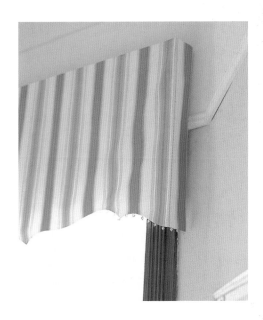

FRENCH COUNTRY REDUX

OPPOSITE: A new maple-finished table is surrounded by chairs with black-and-white seats. A pillow made from toile and checked fabrics echoes the window treatment, while the vases and bowl on the table are the same apple-green as the walls.

For Jane Peterson, bargain hunting is a passion that fills her days without cluttering her home. "I'd rather display just a few good pieces," she says. Her careful eye and pared-down aesthetic sense come through in the Bardstown, Kentucky, home she shares with her husband, Greg, and their two teenage sons. The family designed, built and decorated their home seven years ago. And last year, Jane decided to freshen and lighten up the rooms, giving them a subtle French-country quality. With the tackle-anything frugality that reveals their country roots, they made over the kitchen, as well as the other rooms, themselves.

Since the kitchen, breakfast and sitting areas are linked with the family room Jane painted the spaces with $60 worth of apple-green paint. "It's bright and cheery and it works well with a lot of other colors," says Jane. Here, she paired it primarily with white and black, since she likes to put a touch of black in every room.

Essentially a self-taught sewer who has built her talent into a home-based business, Jane created the window treatments and accessories that complement family antiques and adopted treasures. For the valances, Jane chose black-and-white toile with accents in checks, repeating the combination in pillows and seat covers. Jane and Greg bought an already finished dining set at an unfinished-furniture shop—another staple for bargain hunters. Jane covered the chair seats to match the valances. For other thrifty shoppers, Jane advises buying only those things that you

OPPOSITE: An empty corner in the breakfast room was put to good use with a small built-in desk and storage cabinet made of the same wood used in the kitchen.

RIGHT: Son Andrew helped Jane pick out the wallpaper for the backsplash.

ABOVE: Dark sage walls that closed in the kitchen were revived with apple-green paint, making a tasteful foil for the honey-maple cabinetry. A checked wallpaper with French words decorates the backsplashes. "I prefer wallpaper because you can change it easily and it wears very well," Jane says.

THE TAB

Apple-green paint and supplies	$60.00
Backsplash wallpaper	40.00
Chair-cover fabric	30.00
Window treatments	150.00
TOTAL	$280.00

know you have a home for. "If you buy something based on what you might do, you probably won't ever use it," she says.

A small home office, adjacent to the breakfast area, is used for paying bills and keeping track of school schedules. The area includes a 1920s-style phone and delicate wrought-iron plate hanger, which displays ironstone dishware.

RIGHT: Combining two valances can double the style impact *(see pp. 112–113 for instructions)*. Beneath this toile fabric edged with fringe, another valance peeks through. Its black-and-white check pattern complements the kitchen backsplash. Wrought-iron plate holders and white ironstone plates match the black-and-white color scheme that "pops" next to the apple-green walls, Jane says.

TIMELINE

- Planning . . . . **4 hours**
- Shopping . . . . **4 hours**
- Painting . . . . **3 hours**
- Applying wallpaper backsplash . . . . **1 hour**
- Covering chair seats . . . . **2 hours**
- Making window treatments . . . . **10 hours**

ABOVE: Black-and-white snapshots of the
couple's sons, displayed in a variety of frames,
were the first things hung in the house.
They hold pride of place on the wall
between the kitchen and the family room.

ALL-AMERICAN CHARM

Susan and Andy Carpenter and their young daughters, Eva and Lucy, love spending mornings together in the kitchen/breakfast room of their 100-year-old suburban Colonial home in Somerset County, New Jersey. One of their favorite aspects of the room is the view. "The rolling meadow outside the windows makes us feel like we're in the country," says Susan. But since the windows face east, the intense morning sunlight streaming through the four large windows in the breakfast nook was overwhelming.

"Andy loves to be able to look outside at the view," Susan says. An art director for a large publishing group, Andy conceded the windows needed shades, but he also had strong views on color and style. He didn't want them to be too fussy and he wanted them to complement the colors of the family's Turkish rugs. Fortunately, Susan, a marketing consultant for museums, shared his point of view. But she was certain that the window treatments would be a good addition to the house since they would help control the light and glare and make the rooms look more finished and intimate. So, working with Jean Nayar, the editor of Woman's Day Special Interest Publications' *Budget Decorating Ideas* magazine, the couple set out to develop treatments for the breakfast nook and adjoining kitchen.

Susan and Andy are drawn to bright primaries, which they felt would set off the family's contemporary art. Jean worked with

BEFORE

ABOVE: The accent colors in the graphically patterned Turkish carpet in the breakfast nook drove the color direction for the window treatments.

OPPOSITE: Accented with pristine grosgrain ribbon trim, Roman shades *(see p. 113 for instructions)* with self-valances add a complementary note of cheer to the adjoining breakfast nook.

What They Loved
- The sunny quality of the room.
- The great views of the greenery outdoors.
- The spaciousness of the open-plan room.

What They Hated
- The fact that sometimes the room could be too sunny (the room faces east and the rising sun comes in at eye level).
- The inability to control light because of a lack of window treatments.
- The lack of color and pattern.

TIMELINE

- Measuring windows. . . . . ½ hour
- Reviewing design ideas . . . . ¾ hour
- Designing window treatments . . . . 3 hours
- Searching for and choosing fabrics. . . . . 3 hours
- Calculating yardage, ordering fabric . . . . 1½ hours
- Fabricating window treatments . . . . 30 hours
- Purchasing and cutting lumber. . . . . 2 hours
- Installing Roman shades . . . . 2 hours
- Purchasing and installing curtain rod with balloon shade . . . . . . 1 hour

ABOVE: A bare, wide east-facing window topped with a fanlight offered great views of the landscape but let in too much light.

OPPOSITE: A gathered shade—in an upbeat, classic plaid—permits views outside, but adds to the kitchen a touch of softness that Susan desired. It also helps mute the harsh morning light.

the pair to refine design ideas, offer fabric choices and assist with fabrication and installation. Together, a consensus quickly emerged. The couple chose crisp Roman shades in a blue-and-white plaid for the eating area and a fluffy gathered shade over the sink in the kitchen to soften the window without obscuring the view. The Roman shades sport custom trim of wide grosgrain, which Susan desired. Now that the window treatments are in place, Susan and Andy also realize that they help retain heat in winter, keep hot air out in summer and protect fragile art from the ravages of sunlight.

TAB

17 yards of fabric	**$510.00**
50 yards of ribbon	**83.00**
17 yards of lining	**51.00**
Thread and sewing sundries	**15.00**
Lumber	**8.00**
Curtain rod and mounting hardware	**8.00**
Wood screws	**1.50**
TOTAL	**$676.50**

FINISHING TOUCHES

Adding lining to treatments provides many benefits: It protects the decorative fabric from fading from sunlight, allows your treatment to hang more gracefully and improves its heat-retention abilities.

Make sure the fiber content of the lining fabric is the same as that of the decorative one. That will make the treatment easier to clean. And make sure it's the same width, too, so you won't have extra seams to deal with.

Sew trims to the top of a treatment before you add the lining, so the stitch marks will be hidden.

Before sewing on a trim, glue it in place instead of pinning. That way, you avoid damaging the trim with hole marks or pulls.

For trims placed on curved edges, choose a trim that will bend without buckling, such as a gimp, a flat braid or fabric strips cut on the bias.

Sew on ribbons or trims with tiny zigzag stitches with transparent thread on both sides of the trim because this stitch won't pucker.

FARMHOUSE FANTASY

ABOVE: Shar rejected the old kitchen layout and felt that the window was unrelated to the style of the house.

OPPOSITE: Original beadboard lay behind ceiling panels that Shar and David Cipriano removed. The cabinets—a mix of semicustom units from a home center plus custom millwork crafted to fit specific needs—add function and charm. Crown molding and nickel-plated door and drawer pulls give the cabinetry a custom look. Shar designed the barstool covers *(see p. 115 for instructions)* and had them made from discount fabrics by an upholsterer friend.

Long before they were married, Shar and David Cipriano used to drive by a charming little cottage with a covered porch in Gresham, Oregon, fantasizing how it might be theirs one day. When it finally did go on the market, the couple just happened to be married and house hunting, and they bought it on the spot. During the next 15 years they made cosmetic changes, saving the most challenging space—the kitchen—for last. "What I really wanted," Shar recalls, "was an add-on that included a kitchen/family room, but soon realized that would cost $100,000." Even when she scaled back, the bids were daunting. "I offered to get the materials myself," she says, "but I still got bids of $30,000 to $65,000. I felt my wish list shrinking before my eyes. So, I decided to scrimp on things that didn't really matter and go for things I couldn't give up." What she wanted most was more light, more-efficient work space and gracious comfort. By taking on the designer and contractor roles herself, she got all of that but spent less than $16,000.

Gone was the U-shaped plan that made the 18½ x 19-foot space inefficient to work in. And gone, too, was a window centered over the sink—a 1970s implant and the room's only source of natural light—that was glaringly out of keeping with the style of a house built in 1918. Shar's new kitchen design eschewed the traditional work triangle, focusing instead on her own needs as a

ABOVE: The wood stove and wall-hung phone functioned mainly as props in a disorganized space. The fan/ceiling-light fixture came out when the new windows went in.

OPPOSITE: Though it looks built-in, the banquette *(see p. 114 for instructions)* can be removed if the Ciprianos ever want a formal dining setup.

cook. For example, placing the new refrigerator outside that triangle meant she would not be disturbed when her kids came in for snacks or soft drinks. Installing four traditional double-hung windows meant that the kitchen would have abundant sunlight, ventilation and backyard views. Since the Ciprianos' 1,800-square-foot house sits on five acres of land with gardens, an orchard and a pond, there is much to look at and enjoy outdoors.

Shar wanted all-wood window frames, but was stymied by the price. So she compromised, ordering vinyl frames that she had trimmed with wood on the inside. She also compromised in other ways to keep costs down. She wanted beadboard on the walls to match the original ceiling, which had been obscured in a previous remodeling, and bought it on sale for half price. She knew that neither she nor David was up to the task of leveling, then tiling, the floor, so pros were hired. Having taken a tile course at a home center, however, she decided to do the countertops and backsplash herself. She bought inexpensive 3 x 6-inch white tiles and tackled the counters while the pro was at work on the floor. He willingly answered her questions and offered advice. For cabinets, she visited a firm that made semi-

TIMELINE

The Ciprianos' kitchen remodel took four months to build from the time the design was completed.
They did some of the work themselves, but when they needed pros, they hired subcontractors—all at bargain rates.

- Compiling a wish list for the new kitchen . . . . **2 hours**
- Producing a design on paper that both Shar and David were comfortable with . . . . **6 hours**
- Shopping for appliances, tiles, flooring and countertop materials . . . . **6 hours**
- Removing old cabinets, appliances, wallpaper and countertops . . . . **4 hours**
- Exposing the beadboard ceiling, preparing and painting the surface . . . . **4 hours**
- Getting the electrical work done . . . . **4 hours**
- Upgrading the plumbing . . . . **4 hours**
- Removing old window and filling in its opening, cutting new openings, installing new windows . . . . **2 days**
- Preparing and leveling the subfloor . . . . **6 hours**
- Installing new tile on the floor . . . . **1½ days**
- Tiling the counters and the wall behind the antique wood stove . . . . **10 hours**
- Painting the walls and woodwork . . . . **4 hours**
- Selecting fabrics for and designing valance, barstool covers and cushions, and installing them . . . . **8 hours**

What They Loved
- The scale of the room, and the fact that it had the potential to be a charming, comfortable country kitchen.
- The placement of the kitchen in the plan of the house and the possibility of opening the room to views of the backyard.
- The brick chimney, which rooted the room to its post-Victorian origins.

What They Hated
- The '70s and '80s renovations in the kitchen, which did not relate in any way to the style of the house.
- The U-shaped layout of the kitchen.
- The lack of natural light. With only one window, the room was dark, even at midday. Furthermore, the window was a recent implant at odds with the style of the house.

ABOVE: The Ciprianos removed the busy wallpaper, which added to the old kitchen's overall darkness. They transformed the original space without adding an inch.

RIGHT: White subway tile, painted beadboard, cheery floral fabric and nickel hardware combine to give Shar's new kitchen fresh farmhouse-inspired style.

custom units for large developers. She bought unfinished maple units at a bargain price, then asked a carpenter to blend them with the few custom units she wanted: a wall cabinet, a wall-hung plate rack and a chest to place near the banquette. The carpenter also cut the butcher block that tops the island, whose legs were made from cut-down stair rails that Shar found for a good price at a home center.

For lighting, she visited a store catering to contractors and was offered a discount because the Ciprianos own an excavation company. To her dismay, Shar found the same lights in a catalog for less than half the price she had paid. "I returned them and got my money back," she says. What was the key to her success? "Patience," she says. "If you have it, you can end up with the dream kitchen you may think you can't afford."

THE TAB

Appliances	$3,652.00
Carpentry	3,200.00
Semicustom base cabinets	1,520.00
Electrician	1,300.00
Floor-tile installation	1,243.00
Floor tile	700.00
Plate rack and chest	500.00
Tile for counter, backsplash, stove wall, baking area	460.00
Cushions, pillows and valance, plus labor	400.00
Custom wall cabinet, appliance garage, hood	400.00
Farmhouse sink	400.00
Maple butcher-block counter	400.00
4 windows	350.00
4 stair rails used as island legs	300.00
Plumber	300.00
Sink faucet	139.00
Beadboard paneling	120.00
Light fixtures	114.00
Cabinet hardware	107.00
Antique banquette table	100.00
Custom wood trim	80.00
Paint	75.00
TOTAL	**$15,860.00**

TOP: A cabinet-filled niche beside the refrigerator serves as the coffee corner. The semicustom base cabinets neatly contain the built-in microwave oven.

ABOVE: A niche carved out between wall-mounted cabinets near the sink house a small television. When Shar and her family aren't watching it, doors conceal it.

LEFT: Shar put every square inch of her new kitchen to use, including this space under the stairs, which now serves as a bake area, where a bathroom towel bar with S-hooks holds baking utensils.

OPPOSITE: Space under the stairs, formerly a clumsy closet, became a baking area for Shar. Despite the sloping ceiling, the tile counter's 35-inch depth gives her ample room for rolling out dough. Shar suspended an inexpensive bathroom towel bar from a wood shelf wedged into the triangle and added S-hooks to hold kitchen gear.

ABOVE: A mum-filled antique bread bin stands where the original wood stove had been. The Ciprianos found an antique model in mint condition and had it vented through the ceiling. The brick chimney now provides space for storing cut firewood and some cookware.

ABOVE: A vintage toaster, Fiestaware pitchers, vintage salt and pepper shakers and a framed painting contribute to the color scheme and the charm of the room.

A TOUCH OF PROVENCE

BEFORE

OPPOSITE: In the guest room, Ann made a simple headboard from plywood wrapped with batting and fabric. She also painted milk cartons white and turned them into end tables. Salvaged shutters frame the bed. Ann hot-glued ribbon to the ready-made shades. *(See p. 115 for instructions for the trimmed gingham bedskirt.)*

Ann Pederson doesn't cook or sew, but give her a paintbrush and she's a creative wizard. The best evidence of her talent is her own suburban Virginia home, which she shares with her husband, Kirk, and their 4-year-old son, Ian. The house is new, so Ann, who prefers the weathered farmhouse look of her native Illinois, set out to change it with a combination of flea-market finds, some clever fabric ideas, and a little bit of paint.

Except for sewing projects, which her mother, an interior designer, tackles, Ann does most of the work herself. In this guest room, she painted walls a sunny yellow and added generous touches of black with accessories and fabrics. All of her rooms, including this guest room, also feature a touch of toile—a look Ann considers timeless. "You can pair the pattern with checks or stripes and they all look good," she says. Here she used a mix of toile patterns on the lampshade, valances and pillow covers—as well as on the wallpapered ceiling. A black-and-white checked bedskirt—trimmed with a black border—complements the airy toiles while anchoring the bed.

Ann's window treatments are clean-lined and contemporary. She prefers shades that roll up easily so you can enjoy the view. In this room, she glued a checked ribbon border onto the shades to add emphasis and covered the tops of the windows with simple gathered toile valances. Splashes of yellow linens and blankets add shots of cheer to the pulled-together room.

ABOVE: The garden room, where Ann and Kirk have morning coffee, is also another guest room. To keep views open, Ann gathered and attached unhemmed brown toile to metal finials between windows. She also wallpapered the ceiling in a beadboard-patterned paper.

TIMELINE

- Planning . . . . **8 hours**
- Shopping . . . . **14 hours**
- Making bedskirt . . . . **6 hours**
- Painting room . . . . **8 hours**
- Painting crates to make tables . . . . **4 hours**
- Making window treatments for both rooms . . . . **10 hours**
- Making headboard . . . . **4 hours**
- Having wallpaper installed . . . . **16 hours**

THE TAB FOR TWO ROOMS

Toile wallpaper (materials and labor)	$400.00
Beadboard wallpaper (materials and labor)	490.00
Slipcovered chairs	500.00
Bedskirt (materials and labor)	250.00
Lampshades	36.00
Paint for side tables	20.00
Matelassé coverlet	39.00
Chandelier (used leftover paint)	70.00
Valance and draped treatments (fabric, finials and supplies)	150.00
Headboard (fabric and supplies)	50.00
Brown end tables	80.00
Cedar chest	50.00
TOTAL	**$2,135.00**

What She Loved
- The large windows.
- The abundance of natural light.
- The great view.

What She Hated
- The fact that the windows are so large that no matter where you place the bed, you block a window.
- The difficulty in making the bed in the yellow room.

The basics of Ann's rooms include neutral or crisp colored walls, easy-care fabrics and a creative rethinking of materials. She also favors washable white slipcovers—for quick cleanups, she simply sprays them with a bleach mixture before washing. And she paints most furniture, from her earliest acquisitions to the latest flea-market finds, white, black or with a faux finish. Evidence of these approaches can be clearly seen in the garden room, which doubles as another guest room. Here, two comfy chairs sport easy-care slipcovers and fluffy pillows and provide a place to relax and enjoy a cup of coffee in the morning. Recycled candlesticks add interest and character to the top of a low storage element in front of a window.

Even though she doesn't sew, Ann doesn't let that stop her from using fabric creatively. Because she enjoys the views from this room and because she also favors simple window treatments, she opted to leave the windows bare here, but added a touch of softness to the gaps between the windows by draping floor-length swaths of brown and ivory fabric over finials she simply mounted into the wall near the tops of the windows. By applying a wallpaper with a whitewashed beadboard pattern on the ceiling, Ann added an extra touch of airy country freshness to the room, keeping the ambience pristine yet relaxed.

COUNTRY COMFORT

In Ann Pederson's own master bedroom, comfort is key. The basics of this room include neutral walls, easy-care fabrics and a creative rethinking of materials. With its essentially neutral backdrop, Ann uses fabrics and linens to give the room a totally different look in warm-and-cold weather seasons—here it's fitted in its autumn garb.

Since her mother is an interior designer, Ann grew up surrounded by swatches and samples. Ann recalls running a fledgling decorating business as an elementary school student. "My first project was painting a window shade in my room," says Ann. Today, she runs Posh Rooms, a successful home styling and decorating business, from her office in her family room, where clients can relax and see Ann's work firsthand.

Ann's mother created the fringed round table topper—the only touch of toile in this scheme—and the bullion-fringed bedskirt after Ann painted the walls in a pale buttercream neutral. Ann also refinished key pieces of salvaged furniture and added an eclectic array of accents. Ann paints most furniture, from her earliest acquisitions to the latest flea-market finds, white, black or with a faux look. The nightstand next to her bed was a flea-market find, which Ann painted in ivory, then washed with a glaze to give it character. In keeping with her taste for touches of black, she spray-painted some metal rose pulls black before attaching them to the nightstand's drawers.

BEFORE

OPPOSITE: Above the master bed, a flea-market shelf holds accessories, which Ann changes with the seasons. Ann fashioned ready-made tablecloths into draperies, while her mother pieced together the bullion-fringed bedskirt from two twin-size ruffles *(see p. 116 for instructions)*.

TIMELINE

- Planning . . . . **5 hours**
- Shopping . . . . **14 hours**
- Making bedskirt from 2 twin bedskirts . . . . **4 hours**
- Painting room . . . . **8 hours**
- Painting/finishing dresser . . . . **6 hours**
- Making drapes . . . . **8 hours**
- Mounting shelf, arranging furniture . . . . **3 hours**

In lieu of a headboard, a shelf above the bed—topped with potted topiaries and other collectibles—stands in as a kind of mantel that gives the bed presence, as do a bevy of fluffy pillows covered in a range of fabrics in different colors, patterns and textures.

In general, Ann favors window treatments that are simple and low-cost. In this room, finding window treatments to fit the French doors was problematic, so Ann fashioned the autumn-weather draperies here from a pair of tablecloths, adding tasseled, clip-on rings and trim to give them a custom look.

The colors in the window treatments have inspired the hues in the other fabric elements in the room—from the lampshades and the pillows to the table topper and bed linens—tying the disparate patterns together and imbuing the serene room with shots of warmth that attract the eye.

Currently, Ann is contemplating a few finishing touches—perhaps the shelf above the bed will get a wash of ivory paint when she's ready to transform it for spring.

Here are a few of Ann's favorite ways to make a room both pretty and practical:

Celebrate oft-neglected spaces. "Even on our front porch, I've put billowy mosquito-net curtains on the columns, a soft rug and pillows on the chairs, even a floor lamp. Now, it's a room we can use."

Think creatively. "I couldn't find a tray large enough to use on our living room ottoman, so I made one from an antique picture frame. I change the fabric under the glass with the seasons."

Cherish your history. Dedicate an empty wall to a display of black-and-white family photos. "By our stairs, I have family photos that span a century," says Ann.

Bring in a touch of the outdoors. At night, an outdoor fixture brightens what Ann calls her garden room. "I also like the look of geraniums indoors."

Use rooms in ways that work for your family. "Nothing says you have to use a formal dining room just for dining—use it as a playroom or sitting room, if that's what you need."

THE TAB

Fabric for bedskirts	$28.00
Dresser	80.00
5 metal knobs	35.00
Side table and tablecloth	75.00
Paint for tables	50.00
2 black wicker chairs	138.00
Vintage mirror (flea market find)	50.00
Vintage shelf (flea market find)	50.00
Area rug	199.00
TOTAL	$705.00

ABOVE: A flea-market find, this side table was decorated by Ann to match the colors of the room (see p. 116 for instructions).

SERENE SANCTUARY

Their house was a 50-year-old Colonial in Maplewood, New Jersey, and it was covered with faux-paint finishes, when Bob Hugel and his wife, Leah Bossio, an art director at Woman's Day Special Interest Publications, bought it. "We took no time off to fix it up," explains Leah. "We just painted everything white and moved in four years ago."

Over time, they began making modest improvements in every room—except their own. Recently, with a $500 budget and a little help from designer and stylist Ingrid Leess, the couple turned their bedroom into a warm, inviting sanctuary. "We made very few purchases, using mostly what Bob and Leah owned," says Ingrid. "Mainly we edited the room." After choosing a pale grayish blue-green wall paint, Ingrid suggested a new furniture plan that placed the bed opposite the window wall and included curtains on improvised rods hung a few inches above the windows—"to push up the ceiling height," she says.

A few fresh new color-coordinated accents and some simple do-it-yourself accessories, including a headboard made from a tatami mat, curtain rods created from bound bamboo, a folding screen covered with grass cloth wallpaper, and a pair of table lamps made with clear glass bottles as bases—give the bedroom custom character at a price that was easy on their wallets. The best part: With Ingrid's help, Leah and Bob managed to get the entire job done in just one long weekend.

BEFORE

OPPOSITE: Instead of reusing the headboard, the designer bought a precut 30 x 60-inch woven mat and improvised a decorative substitute (see p. 117 for instructions). She hung it on the wall with picture hooks. Then, with two Make-a-Lamp kits (see p. 117 for instructions), she fashioned pretty bedside lamps from two inexpensive, tall, clear-glass bottles topped with crisp shades.

What They Loved

- Spaciousness. Having lived in a one-bedroom apartment until their first child was a toddler, they found a 12½ x 16-foot bedroom of their own a luxury.
- High-quality furniture. The fruitwood bedroom set with Oriental touches was a hand-me-down from Leah's parents. "We felt lucky to have it," she says.
- Natural light. With three windows, the room is flooded with sunshine on most mornings.
- Closet space. "In our apartment we had only one closet," Leah recalls. "My husband, my son and I shared it. So for Bob and me to have our own separate closets, with built-in shelves, feels special."

What They Hated

- The nondescript decor. "Other parts of the house needed attention," says Leah. "Our room was an afterthought—very cluttered and messy. We really needed someone to help us pull it together."
- The undecorated bed. Discount-store bed linens that were boring and blah—truly unappealing.
- The lack of serenity. "It was never a nice place to relax in," Leah says, "and it was depressing to wake up there. We longed for a comfortable space to retreat to at the end of the day."

THE TAB

2 hollow-core doors	$39.98
1 hinge	3.27
1 lampshade	24.99
1 wallpaper double-roll for doors	28.00
2 vases	26.94
2 decorative boxes	20.98
1 bamboo mat for headboard	29.99
1 bedspread	39.99
2 floor pillows	36.98
2 Make-a-Lamp kits	13.38
3 bamboo-stakes bundles for curtain rods	5.91
3 pairs of tab curtains	38.97
6 curtain brackets	12.00
3 bamboo roll-up blinds	20.97
1 chair slipcover	18.99
4 picture frames with mats	67.97
4 photo enlargements	8.00
2 gallons of wall paint	30.00
Chrome spray paint for mirror frame	5.49
TOTAL	**$472.80**

BEFORE

ABOVE: The top of the bedroom console had been a catchall for the TV, magazines and other items.

OPPOSITE: To give the console greater presence in the updated space, Leah enlarged family photos, mounted them in prematted frames and hung them on the wall above the piece.

BEFORE

ABOVE: A mishmash of unrelated objects on top of the dresser detract from its beauty.

RIGHT: Newly framed family photos and old and new accents complement the color scheme.

OPPOSITE: To soften the look of the mirrored closet doors, Ingrid covered the front of two hollow-core doors in a grass cloth-textured wallpaper, then hinged the doors to create a decorative screen.

BELOW: Ingrid improvised curtain rods by binding together three bamboo poles, which subtly enhance the Asian-influenced decor (see p. 117 for instructions).

DO'S AND DON'TS FOR CREATING AN INVITING BEDROOM

Do drench your walls with rich, warm, soothing color, especially if your bedroom has windows facing north.

Don't forget to load a pale room with plenty of texture like nubby fabrics, shiny pillows and woven throws to produce some subtle warmth.

Do include family pictures. A bookcase filled with photos—in stylish but not necessarily identical frames—adds a decorative and very personal touch to a bedroom.

Don't neglect accessories. Even a wastebasket makes a difference. Instead of a boring plastic receptacle, opt for a charming wicker basket or painted canister.

Do pay attention to the first spot you see when you enter the room, and arrange a vignette there. Place a chair with a beautiful pillow, say, or a stunning piece of vertical art there, so you'll have something attractive for your eye to land on every day.

Don't obsess about furniture. Pieces don't have to match as long as they're first cousins. Search thrift shops for furnishings that have complementary lines. A pretty king-size sheet can disguise a chair until you're ready to reupholster, and paint works wonders.

LEFT: A soothing color scheme of soft browns, white and blue keeps the room relaxed, while a mix of silky-smooth and textured surfaces adds visual interest.

BELOW AND BOTTOM: A mix of new do-it-yourself accents, such as the lamp made from a clear glass bottle and topped with a recycled shade and old curios and artworks found in other rooms in the house kept costs low.

TIMELINE

- Surveying the room and taking measurements . . . . **2 hours**
- Doing inventory of the attic and basement. . . . . **3 hours**
- Shopping . . . . **1 day**
- Prepping and painting . . . . **1 day**
- Crafting bedside lamps and the folding screen, framing photos, spray-painting mirror frame . . . . **½ day**
- Rearranging furniture . . . . **2 hours**
- Installing window treatments, dressing the bed, hanging pictures, pulling it all together . . . . **2 hours**

OPPOSITE: A spare dining chair topped with a ready-made slipcover pulls up to a table from Leah and Bob's attic that serves as both a desk and a dressing table. The mirror was another attic find. Its frame, treated to a coat of chrome spray paint, gleams like silver.

What They Loved

- The scale. The size of the room and the placement of its windows suggested that the bedroom had strong decorating potential.
- The storage. There are two closets—and both are capacious enough to hold everything the Carpenters need to stash.
- The natural light. Tall, large windows let in plenty of sunlight and provide splendid views of the country landscape.
- The details. The woodwork and paneled wall are original to the house, as is the fireplace with its carved-wood mantel. To keep it from creating an ugly void when not in use, Jean crafted and painted a handsome fireplace screen.

What They Hated

- The lack of warmth. "The walls were a muddy tone, which added to the feeling of coldness," says Susan.
- The lack of cohesiveness. The room was filled with a lot of disparate pieces of furniture that, Susan says, "just happened to wind up there."
- The location of the TV. The Carpenters wanted a television in their bedroom but hated having the set placed so prominently. Susan says that Jean's idea of hiding it in an armoire was "a lovely solution."

BEFORE

TIMELINE

- Inventorying the room and editing existing furnishings. . . . . **2 hours**
- Measuring the room, the furniture and the fireplace . . . . **2 hours**
- Designing the headboard, slipcovers and window treatments. . . **8 hours**
- Choosing new furnishings and painting unfinished pieces . . . . . **6 hours**
- Moving furniture out and painting walls and woodwork . . . . . . **9 hours**
- Shopping for lumber, supplies and decorative accents . . . . **5 hours**
- Fabricating soft-goods pieces. . . . . **80 hours**
- Making the headboard. . . . . **3 hours**
- Moving in all the furniture. . . . . **1 hour**
- Constructing and painting fireplace screen . . . . **3½ hours**
- Installing window treatments and hanging pictures . . . . **4 hours**

THE TAB

Unpainted armoire and nightstands	$1,394.00
Fabric for curtains and slipcovers	1,369.00
New comforter and throw pillow	184.00
6½ gallons of paint and primer	130.00
Curtain lining fabric and notions	100.00
Batting and foam for headboard	91.00
New drawer and door pulls for nightstands, armoire	60.00
Plywood and lumber	40.00
Picture stretchers for fireplace screen	24.00
Paintbrushes, rollers and painter's tape	21.00
Spray glue for batting	12.00
Hinges for fireplace screen	12.00
Nails and picture hooks	6.00
Gilding paint for picture frames	3.00
TOTAL	**$3,446.00**

LEFT: Without a decorative fire screen in front of it, the fireplace looked like a black hole. The hodgepodge of photos on the mantel was moved to another location and replaced with decorative pieces that bring out the best in the mantel.

OPPOSITE: Using plywood and picture stretchers, plus two coats of paint, Jean made a hinged fire screen (see p. 118 for instructions) for the Adam-style fireplace. Above it, on the mantel, is a ceramic urn that had once stood on the mantel in Susan's great-grandparents' home.

ABOVE: A new monogrammed pillow *(see p. 118 for instructions)* lends new life to an old slipper chair, which, along with the ottoman, got new slipcovers with box pleats sewn by a friend. Susan replaced the hardware on a chest that had been in her family for generations. Then she gilded the frames of the artwork flanking the mirror.

BEFORE

OPPOSITE: The bordered curtains were designed and sewn by a friend *(see p. 120 for instructions)*, and Susan mounted them on existing wooden rods raised to crown-molding height for drama. The TV now resides in the armoire, an unfinished piece that Susan painted and sealed. Andy painted the thrift-shop table Chinese red.

CRISP AND CLEAN

Shar Cipriano is an interior designer whose firm, Reflections of You, in Gresham, Oregon, is known for helping clients keep the lid on costs. In remodeling her own kitchen, she put her practiced skills to the test—and succeeded beautifully. Next, she and her husband, David, tackled the bathroom. Since it's the only bath in their three-bedroom house—a bungalow built on five acres in 1918—and since it must be shared by the couple *and* their two teenage children, it had to be completely practical as well as attractive.

"The old bath had a look of the 1980s," says Shar. "It had dark wallpaper and dark oak trim. It was part of a renovation done before we bought the house, and it felt kind of Victorian." The scale of the room, with its tall, vaulted ceiling, was a plus; at 7½ x 9½ feet it was just right for the family's needs. And the arrangement of elements—sink, toilet, tub/shower—was efficient. But David agreed with Shar that everything in the bath needed replacing.

"The two of us gutted the entire space," Shar recalls. It was a job perfectly suited to David, who owns an excavation business in which Shar is a partner. Having done the demolition work themselves, the Ciprianos felt they could afford to hire a carpenter to do the finish work—framing the new tub surround, applying beadboard to the walls and trimming the doors with molding that matched what appears in the rest of the house. The

BEFORE

OPPOSITE: The new layout is the same as the old, but tile and fixtures are white, and the fabrics *(see pp. 120–121 for instructions for the shower curtain)* are keyed to the sunlight that pours through the single shuttered window.

LEFT: The vanity, made of plywood-covered 2x4s, proved a simple chore for the Ciprianos' gifted carpenter. Shar finished the job by applying two coats of white paint plus protective polyurethane.

BEFORE

ABOVE: The old bath was as dark as a Victorian parlor, its heavy atmosphere underscored by a dark-stained oak vanity, drab-looking tile and less-than-cheery wallpaper.

What She Loved
- The size and layout of the bathroom and its vaulted ceiling.
- That the bath had already been plumbed for two sinks.
- The recessed ceiling lights that were already in use.
- The large window with a sunny countryside view.
- The potential for creating country-cottage charm.

What She Hated
- The dark and dated decor.
- Oak trim on everything—definitely an 80s look.
- The murky-colored tile, much of it stained with soap scum.
- The shallow bathtub—only 11 inches deep.

craftsman they hired, Steve Brouner, also built the new vanity, using 2 x 4s and sheets of plywood. A local home center supplied the above-counter basin-style sinks that Shar says "give us a bit of a vintage look." She wanted modern conveniences but was determined to keep the room simple yet functional, reminiscent of old farmhouse baths.

Shar not only painted the room herself; she also did the tiling, using 1 x 1-inch hexagonal tiles on the floor and 3 x 6-inch white tiles around the tub/shower, many of them had been left over from the kitchen redo. She reused the white outer curtain from the old bath but wanted a cheery plaid inner curtain she had seen in a home store and bought two. She cut up the

BELOW: Shar says she picked above-counter basins that add farmhouse flavor to a space that otherwise looks refreshingly contemporary.

LEFT: The "Wash" labeled hook unit makes hanging towels an aesthetic experience.

BELOW: A framed picture of Lacey and Cy, the Cipriano children, stands on the top shelf of the niche Shar designed to replace a built-in rack for towels *(see p. 121 for instructions).*

THE TAB

Toilet	$139.00
2 basin-style sinks	412.00
2 sink drains	42.00
Bathtub	340.00
Tub/shower fittings, drain	25.00
Beadboard, wood trim, wood door, 2 cabinet doors	325.00
2 light sconces	90.00
Window	100.00
2 white-painted shutters	250.00
3 x 6-inch wall tile	200.00
1 x 1-inch hexagonal floor tile	230.00
2 adjustable wall mirrors	358.00
2 plaid shower curtains	50.00
Wall-hung towel hooks	40.00
2 steel baskets for towels	20.00
Paint	20.00
Cabinet hardware	10.00
Plumber	300.00
Carpenter	1,090.00
TOTAL	**$4,041.00**

second curtain to create a tieback as well as a deep valance above the shuttered window.

Her most significant improvement involved a niche that previous owners had cut into one wall and trimmed with oak. Within it, like the rungs of a ladder, were a series of towel bars—a practical idea, but the Ciprianos felt the look was strictly '80s. It was Shar's idea to remove the oak trim and all the towel rungs; then she collaborated with her carpenter, who built two open shelves over a closed cupboard—"where we could put the clutter that no one sees," says Shar. She calls it a functional redo that "looks as though it's been there forever."

Every design idea takes time to develop and evolve, and as Shar points out, "planning makes everything run more smoothly." Remodelings can disrupt an entire household. Thus, she adds, "I think patience is extremely important. In the long run it can save you a lot of money."

OPPOSITE: Shar started tiling with white 3 x 6s left over from her kitchen remodeling. She augmented the supply with new purchases plus enough olive-green for an attractive stripe on each wall of the shower. Her new tub, with its 24-inch depth, is more than a foot deeper than its predecessor.

TIMELINE

The Ciprianos planned their bath transformation carefully so the work could be completed in two weeks. It was in use—very carefully—during construction. "No one was allowed to splash," says Shar.

- Removing the old tub, vanity and towel niche . . . . .1 hour
- Removing old tile backsplash and tub surround . . . . .6 hours
- Installing new tub frame and the hardiboard for tiling . . . . . . .5 hours
- Putting in the new tub, framing in the niche . . . . .6 hours
- Tiling the shower wall and tub deck . . . . .4 days, 6 hours each
- Installing new window, door and trim . . . . .8 hours
- Installing beadboard, cabinet doors and wood shelves . . . . . .12 hours
- Installing tub, connecting sinks and shower . . . . .4 hours
- Putting up sconce lights and twin mirrors . . . . .3 hours
- Painting beadboard and upper walls . . . . .2 days, 4 hours each
- Tiling floor . . . . .2 days, 8 hours each

ABOVE: Instead of towel bars, Shar used gym-style steel racks for washcloths and guest towels. She found them inexpensive and easy to slide in and out of vanity shelving.

GET THE
LOOK

ANN'S FAMILY ROOM
Tin Ceiling Tile Frame

SKILL LEVEL: BEGINNER

MATERIALS: Tin ceiling tile; yardstick; 4-inch-wide pieces of barn wood or other distressed wood, about 1-inch-thick; ¼-inch square strips of balsa or other wood; handsaw; miter box; wood glue; C-clamps; staple gun; wood primer; black acrylic paint; paintbrushes; hammer; ¾-inch brads; picture-hanging kit with wire

DIRECTIONS

1. Measure tile; cut four pieces of wood to these measurements plus 8 inches. Using miter box, cut each end of each piece at a 45-degree angle, so that one side of each board equals length of one side of the tile. Cut four strips of ¼-inch square wood into pieces equal in length to one side of tile minus ¼ inch.

2. Glue wood pieces together at ends to form frame; clamp each corner until glue dries, forming frame. Fit the ¼-inch-square strips of wood around interior of front of frame, starting at one corner, fitting next strip in the ¼-inch gap, positioning it perpendicular to the first, and gluing both pieces in place as you go. Repeat with the remaining two strips, gluing in place and letting dry completely. Use staple gun to add two or three staples across backs of frame seams.

3. Coat frame with primer; let dry. Apply two or more coats of paint to frame, letting dry after each coat.

4. Place front of ceiling tile into frame from the back; tap brads into interior edge of frame behind the tile at the corners leaving part of the brads extending to secure tile in place. Tap in more brads in this manner along sides, spacing them about 6 inches apart.

5. Attach hooks from hanging kit to back of frame, near each side edge. Follow kit directions to attach wire between hooks.

Ceiling Border

SKILL LEVEL: BEGINNER

MATERIALS: Roll of patterned wallpaper or wallpaper border; metal yardstick; pencil; cutting mat; craft knife; wallpaper paste; wallpaper brush; sponge

DIRECTIONS

1. Measure and mark lines along a strip of wallpaper, spacing them 2 inches apart. Mark more lines perpendicular to first set of lines, again spacing them 2 inches apart.

2. Place paper on cutting mat; using knife and yardstick, cut out paper squares.

3. Measure the length of each segment of ceiling you plan to border to determine how many squares, placed on the diagonal, you'll need to create the border. A 2-inch square measures 3 inches across the diagonal. So to determine the number of squares you'll need, calculate the border length in inches and divide by 3. For a 120-inch-long wall, for example, you'll need 40 squares. For a fractional number, round up to the nearest whole number.

4. Mark the center of the ceiling along one wall. Follow manufacturer's directions to mix wallpaper paste. Brush paste onto back of a square. Align the center point of the square with the center of the ceiling and press the square on the diagonal to the ceiling. Repeat this process with other squares as you work toward each corner of room, aligning the side points of the squares and spacing them evenly. Trim corner squares as needed to align flush with the ceiling at the ends.

5. While paste is still wet, use damp sponge to smooth squares and remove any air bubbles. Let dry.

6. Repeat along other walls in the same manner.

JANE AND GREG'S FAMILY ROOM
Balloon Shade With Contrasting Pleats

SKILL LEVEL: INTERMEDIATE

MATERIALS: Cotton fabrics in a toile and a check (or contrasting prints of your choice); tape measure; chalk marking pencil; scissors; lining fabric; pins; coordinating cord piping; matching threads; sewing machine; hand-sewing needle; ½-inch plastic rings; ½-inch polyester twill tape; 1 x 2-inch mounting board, cut 2 inches wider than outer width of window frame and painted to match frame; two small "L" brackets and hardware; two screw eyes; shade cord and pull; awning cleat and mounting hardware; hand drill with drill and screwdriver bits; heavy-duty staple gun and staples

DIRECTIONS

1. Measure the width of the mounting board; add 3 inches to this measurement. Measure the inside window height; add 10 inches to this measurement. Measure, mark and cut a piece of the main fabric to these dimensions. For the lining, add 16 inches to the cut width of the shade. Measure, mark and cut a piece of lining fabric (or toile) to this width by the cut height of the shade. Cut two 9-inch-wide pieces of contrasting fabric to cut shade height for pleats.

2. Pin the cord piping to each long edge of the contrasting fabric, with right sides facing and raw edges even. Using a zipper foot, baste close to the base of the cording.

3. Cut the shade fabric lengthwise about one-quarter of the way in from each long side edge, to divide shade fabric in three sections. With right sides facing and raw edges even, pin a pleat section between each side and center section of shade; using a zipper foot, stitch together the long edges with a ½-inch seam.

4. Pin the shade to the lining, with right sides facing and raw edges even. Stitch around all edges with a ½-inch seam, leaving a 15-inch opening at the center along the top. Turn the shade right side out; press. Slip-stitch the opening closed.

5. To form the pleats, fold both the front and lining layers of the shade to form a box pleat along the contrasting fabric

inserts (see Glossary on page 123 for instructions on how to form a box pleat); pin in place with the edges of the cording aligned; press. Stitch along the top and bottom of the shade to secure the box pleat in place.

6. Mark the tape placement on the wrong side of the shade—it should be placed along the center of each pleat, starting 3 inches from the upper edge and ending 1 inch from the lower edge. Stitch close to the edges of the tape.

7. With the wrong side up, mark the ring placement on the tape. Place the first rings near the lower edges of the tapes and end the rings near the upper edge of tapes; space the remaining rings about 10 inches apart between these rings. Hand-stitch the rings to the tape.

8. Align the upper edge of the wrong side of the shade with the back edge of the top of the mounting board; staple in place, wrapping the shade carefully around the corners.

9. Mark the placement of the screw eyes on the underside of board, directly above each row of rings. Use the drill to make small pilot holes; screw the eyes in place.

10. Cut two pieces of cord, one twice the height of the window, the other two and a half times the height of the window. Decide whether cords will hang on the left or the right side of the window, then tie the longer cord to the bottom ring on the opposite side and the shorter one on the other bottom ring. String the cords up through each ring in each row, then through the screw eye above. String the opposite cord through the screw eye on the cord side, so both cords go through this screw eye and hang on one side of the shade.

11. Mark the placement of the brackets near the ends of the mounting board and drill pilot holes into the board. Screw brackets onto the board, then screw the board over the window and into the wall so the shade hangs in front. With the shade lowered, adjust the cord length so the tension is equal on both cords, then thread on the pull and knot the cords together about three-quarters of the way down shade. Trim the excess cord below the knot.

12. Screw the cleat to the wall about halfway down the window length; pull the cords to raise the shade to the desired level, adjusting the pleats so the checked fabric shows, then wrap the cords around the cleat to secure the shade.

Lampshade

SKILL LEVEL: BEGINNER

MATERIALS: Purchased lampshade; nonflammable fringe trim; hot-glue gun

DIRECTIONS

1. Place the shade on the lamp to make the fringe easier to apply.

2. Starting at the seam on the upper edge of the shade, apply a 2-inch-long bead of glue. Press the fringe onto the glue.

3. In this manner, continue applying glue and pressing the fringe into place along the entire upper edge of the shade; trim the end of the fringe so ends butt at the seam.

4. Apply the fringe to the lower edge of shade.

SUSAN AND ANDY'S FAMILY ROOM
London Shade With Self-Valance

SKILL LEVEL: BEGINNER

MATERIALS: 3½-inch-wide x ½-inch-thick x 4-inch-tall mounting board; tape measure; yardstick; handsaw or circular saw; two small "L" brackets and hardware; striped fabric; chalk marking pencil; scissors; pins; matching thread; sewing machine; hand-sewing needle; ½-inch plastic rings; two screw eyes; shade cord; awning cleat and mounting hardware; hand drill with drill and screwdriver bits; heavy-duty staple gun and staples

NOTE: Sue and Andy's shades came from Smith+Noble, but if you'd like to make one yourself here's how.

DIRECTIONS

1. Measure the window width from outside the frame; add 1 to 3 inches to this measurement depending on how wide you want your shade to be and how much room is available on either side. Measure, mark and cut the mounting board to this length. Determine the placement of the board above the window frame, and mark it on the wall holding up the mounting board and using a carpenter's level. Mark the positions of the "L" brackets on the wall and on the bottom of the mounting board, holding them in place as you do.

2. For the shade, measure the length of the mounting board, and add 9 inches. Measure the window height from the top of the mounting board to the sill; add 4 inches to this measurement. Cut a piece of fabric and a piece of lining to these dimensions. For the self-valance, measure both sides

and the length of the mounting board, add these measurements together, then add 1 more inch. Divide the cut length of the shade by 5 and add 4 inches. Cut a piece of fabric to these dimensions, making sure your pattern matches when the valance is centered over the finished pleated shade. (The finished valance should extend 4 inches on both sides of the shade, which will cover the returns of the mounting board.)

3. Pin the shade to the lining, with right sides facing and raw edges even. Stitch edges with a ½-inch seam, leaving a 15-inch opening at the center along the top. Turn the shade right side out; press. Topstitch the opening closed. Repeat for the valance.

4. About 10 inches from each side edge of shade, form two 2-inch pleats in the shade and pin in place; stitch through all layers to secure pleats at the top and hand-tack the pleats in place at the bottom.

5. With the wrong side up, mark the ring placement on the shade along pleats. Place the first rings near lower edge of the shade and space the remaining rings about 10 inches apart along the pleat ending about 12 inches from the top of the shade. Hand-stitch the rings to the shade only through the first layer of the pleats. Center the valance over the top of the shade, aligning the top edges and topstitch the valance to the shade about ¼ inch from top edge.

6. Align the upper edge of the wrong side of the shade and valance with the back edge of the top of the mounting board; staple in place, carefully folding the valance fabric around the corners to create crisp returns.

7. Mark the placement of the screw eyes on the center of the underside of the board, directly above the rings. Use the drill to make small pilot holes; screw the eyes in place.

8. Cut two pieces of cord, one twice the length of window, the other two and a half times this length. Decide whether cords will hang on the left or the right side of the window, then tie the longer cord to the bottom ring on the opposite side; tie the other cord to the other bottom ring. String the cords up through each ring in each row, then through screw eye above. String the opposite cord through screw eye on cord side. Then string the opposite cord through the screw eye on the cord side, so both cords go through this screw eye and hang on one side of the shade.

9. Using brackets, screw the board over the top of the window. With the shade lowered, adjust the cord length so tension is equal on both cords, then thread the pull onto the cords and knot the cords together about three-quarters of the way down the shade. Trim the excess cord below the knot.

10. Screw the cleat into the window frame or wall about halfway down window length; pull the cords to raise shade to the desired level, then wrap them around the cleat to secure the shade.

PETER'S LIVING ROOM
Painted Floor Lamp

SKILL LEVEL: BEGINNER

MATERIALS: Old pedestal lamp with wood base; protective gloves (optional); paintbrushes; gel paint stripper (optional); soft cotton cloths (optional); wire furniture-stripping brush (optional); 180-grit sandpaper (optional); paint primer; spray paint in desired color; painter's tape; glue (optional); 1 yard 1/2-inch-wide grosgrain ribbon (optional); scissors (optional); seam sealant (optional)

DIRECTIONS

1. Remove shade and any metal fittings from lamp base, if possible.

2. Wearing protective gloves, coat painted wood areas with stripper; allow to set, following manufacturer's directions, then wipe off excess. Use wire brush to remove stripper and paint from carved areas of wood. Reapply stripper to these areas if needed. Wipe stripped wood with soft cloths to remove all residue. If you prefer not to strip the base, you can sand the base instead, completely smoothing any areas where paint is chipped or finish is cracked.

3. Apply primer to all surfaces of wood; let dry.

4. Apply painter's tape to all areas of lamp that will not be painted (any metal fittings which could not be removed, for example). Working in a well-ventilated area with a protected work surface, spray-paint wood surfaces. Apply several light coats to avoid drips; let dry after each coat.

5. Reassemble lamp.

6. Trim shade, if desired. Apply a thin bead of glue around lower edge of shade. Starting at seam, press ribbon around lower edge. Clip excess at seam so the ribbon ends abut. Apply a seam sealant to keep ribbon edges from fraying.

Whipstitched Lampshade

SKILL LEVEL: BEGINNER

MATERIALS: Paper lampshade; tape measure; scissors; leather cording or 1/2- to 1/4-inch-wide ribbon; pencil; hole punch that makes 1/8-inch holes

DIRECTIONS

1. Measure the circumference of the top of your lampshade. Double this measurement and cut a piece of cord or ribbon to this length.

2. Mark equally spaced 3/4- to 1-inch increments around the top of the shade about 1/4 inch to 1/2 inch below rim.

3. Using a hole punch, punch through the shade at each mark.

4. Starting at the seam of the shade, thread the cord through the nearest hole from the outside of the shade to the inside, pulling almost the entire length of the cord through the hole and leaving an 8-inch tail outside the shade.

5. Pull the cord over the rim of the shade and insert through the next hole, continuing to whipstitch around the rim until you reach the final hole.

6. At the seam, tie the two loose ends into a bow or knot and clip the ends to the length you desire.

Framed Map

SKILL LEVEL: BEGINNER

MATERIALS: Sponge paintbrush; decoupage medium; map, or section cut from map, about 4 feet square; 47-inch square of 1/2-inch-thick wood, like pine or medium density fiberboard; 16 feet of 2- to 2 1/2-inch-wide wood lattice; pencil; ruler; handsaw; sandpaper; tack cloth; wood stain in desired color; flat paintbrushes; wood glue; 3/4-inch brads; hammer; polyurethane sealer; two two-hole "D" ring hangers with screws; drill with 1/8-inch bit (optional); screwdriver; picture wire; 50-lb. picture hook

DIRECTIONS

1. Using sponge brush, apply decoupage medium to back of map. Center map on board; smooth from center out to remove any air bubbles and fold excess paper to back of board. Let dry. Apply two or more coats of decoupage medium to front of map, letting dry after each coat.

2. Measure, mark and cut four pieces of wood lattice, each about 1/4 inch longer than board sides, to make frame.

3. Place board facedown on protected work surface. Fit lattice around board so ends fit together tightly; trim lattice as needed. Remove lattice pieces.

4. Sand each lattice piece; wipe off dust with tack cloth. Following manufacturer's instructions, apply one or more coats of stain to each piece as desired to achieve color, letting dry after each coat.

5. Apply glue around edges of board. Place lattice around board again, so that it projects in front of map about 1/8 to 1/4 inch, and one end of each strip is flush with one side of board, and the other end projects from other side of board 1/4 inch. Glue overlapping lattice ends together, then nail together at corners and into edges of board, spacing brads about 6 inches apart along edges to form frame.

6. When glue is dry, apply a coat of polyurethane sealer to frame; let dry.

7. Measure and mark a point on the back of the map about 2 inches in from one side and 1/3 of the way down from the top of the map. Repeat on the other side. Position a "D" ring hanger at these points, so that the bottom hole of the hangers aligns with the point and the "D" ring faces toward the center. Install the screws into the holes. Repeat on the other sides. (Mark the positions of both holes for each hanger, and drill in starter holes about 1/8-inch deep before inserting screws, if desired.)

8. Cut a piece of picture wire about 6 inches longer than the width of the map. Thread wire through rings folding about 3 inches of wire over at ends on each side, knotting and twisting ends around wire.

9. Hammer hook into wall at desired height and hang map.

JUDY AND BOB'S LIVING/FAMILY ROOM
Chair Cushion Cover

SKILL LEVEL: BEGINNER

MATERIALS: 3-inch-thick foam cushion, cut to fit chair seat; tape measure; yardstick; pencil or tailor's chalk; heavy cotton fabric; scissors; pins; matching thread; sewing machine; hand-sewing needle

DIRECTIONS

1. Measure width of cushion in front and back; add 4 inches to these measurements. Measure depth of cushion (from front to back); double this measurement and add 7 inches. Cut fabric to these measurements.

2. Fold the fabric in half, right sides facing, raw short edges matching, pin and sew the short ends together with 1/2-inch seam.

3. Turn the fabric right side out and slide the fabric over the cushion, overlapping long edges in centers of sides of cushion and centering the sewn seam along the back of the cushion.

4. Fold in fabric at each side of cushion, first folding in short ends then folding over long edges, like wrapping a package. On one side, turn under one long edge 1/2 inch, pressing sharply with your fingertips and pin, and position it over the other long edge to conceal all raw sides. Repeat on other side. Slip-stitch close to folded edges to secure fabric and cover cushion completely.

JANE AND GREG'S DINING ROOM
Pleated Valance With Jabots

SKILL LEVEL: INTERMEDIATE

MATERIALS: ½-inch thick x 2-inch wide x 6-inch tall mounting board, cut 4 inches longer than outside window width; tape measure; pencil; hand drill; 2 "L" brackets and mounting hardware; metal yardstick; decorator fabric; coordinating cotton lining fabric; tailor's chalk; scissors; butcher paper; coordinating fringe trim; matching thread; pins; sewing machine; tape; iron and ironing board; staple gun; screwdriver

DIRECTIONS

1. Measure and mark desired placement of valance across window, by holding board and brackets in place and marking placement of brackets on outside of window frame and underside of board.

2. Remove board; drill screw guide holes in board and alongside or above window frame at marks.

3. The height of the finished valance without the jabots should be one-fifth the distance between the top of the valance and the windowsill and its length should be three-fifths the length of the mounting board. For the valance, cut a piece of fabric equal to one-fifth the height from the top of the valance to the windowsill plus 2½ inches by three-fifths the length of the mounting board, plus 10 inches for each 5-inch-wide box pleat, plus 1 inch. (If your fabric is patterned, add the equivalent of the width of either one half or one pattern repeat for each pleat instead of 8 inches.) Your valance should have either three or five pleats depending on how wide your window is. Cut a piece of lining fabric to the same dimensions.

4. The height of the longest part of the finished jabots should be half the height from the top of the valance to the windowsill and the length of each finished jabot across the front of the mounting board should be about one-fifth the length of the mounting board. The length of the unfinished fabric for each jabot should be equal in length to five times 9 inches (the equivalent of three times the width of each 3-inch-wide pleat), plus 7 inches. (That is, if each of five pleats is 3 inches wide, your jabot fabric needs to be 45 inches for the pleats plus 7 inches for the return and seam allowances, or a total of 52 inches long; when pleated, each finished jabot, in this case, would be 15 inches wide plus 6 inches for the return.) The jabot fabric needs to be cut at an angle with the height of one side equal to the height of the unfinished valance and the height of the other side equal to half the height from the top of the valance to the windowsill plus 2½ inches. Mark these dimensions on a piece of butcher paper to make a pattern and cut it out.

5. Pin the pattern to a piece of decorator fabric that's been folded in half and cut out the two pieces of fabric (match

patterns with your valance if necessary). Repeat to cut two pieces of lining for the jabots as well.

6. With right sides facing and raw edges even, pin ends of valance to short ends of jabots and stitch raw edges with ½-inch seams. Repeat with lining. Place lining over valance with jabots, right sides facing and raw edges matching, and pin in place. Stitch raw edges with ½-inch seam, leaving the upper edge open. Trim corners; clip seams. Turn right side out; press. Zigzag stitch the raw edges of the opening closed.

7. With valance faceup, pin fringe along lower edge of valance so it overlaps valance by ½ inch, turning under fringe at ends. Stitch close to upper edge of fringe.

8. Mark fold lines for jabot and valance pleats along upper edge, starting with the first box pleat in the center of the valance, marking other valance box pleats equal distances apart (see Glossary on page 123 for instructions on how to make box pleats, but note that the first fold should be made with wrong side facing since these box pleats face outward). Then mark jabot pleats. Pleat fabric along marks; pin in place. Tape pinned, pleated valance along mounting board to be sure it fits. If not, remove and adjust pleats until it does; then press pleats. On lining side, hand-stitch pleats in place. Remove pins.

9. Press a 2½-inch fold along the top edge of the valance toward the lining side. Using the staple gun, staple the 2-inch folded edge of the valance along the length of the mounting board, starting in the center and folding under the fabric as you turn the corners of the return.

10. Use the screwdriver to mount the brackets to the mounting board, then mount the valance and board above window frame, or across it if you have a window like Jane's.

Decorative Pillows

SKILL LEVEL: BEGINNER

MATERIALS: Pillow forms in desired sizes; tape measure; yardstick; tailor's chalk; upholstery fabrics; scissors; matching thread; cotton cord for piping and 1-inch brush fringe trim; pins; sewing machine with zipper foot; hand-sewing needle; matching buttons

DIRECTIONS

1. For piped pillow, measure length and width of pillow form. Add 1 inch to each measurement; cut two pieces of fabric to these measurements for pillow front and back. Cut remaining fabric into 2-inch-wide bias strips; stitch strips together end to end to make long strip for piping.

2. For buttoned pillow, measure length and width of pillow form. Add 1 inch to each measurement; cut 1 piece of fabric to these measurements for pillow back. For pillow front, add 1 inch to width and 3 inches to length; cut one piece of fabric to these measurements.

3. To make piped pillow, cut fabric 3 inches longer and 1 inch wider than pillow form. Fold piping strip lengthwise over cord, right side out; using a zipper foot, stitch close to base of cord. With right sides facing and raw edges even, pin piping to pillow front. Clip cord to abut where ends meet, and clip and fold over casing on one side of piping to enclose raw edge on other side. Stitch piping to front, close to base of cord. Pin front to back, with right sides facing and raw edges even; stitch together with $\frac{1}{2}$-inch seam, leaving 8-inch opening along one side. Clip corners, turn right side out, insert pillow form and slip-stitch opening closed.

4. To make buttoned pillow, fold front in half crosswise, with wrong sides facing and raw edges even. Stitch 1 inch from fold. Open out flat; press fold to one side. Stitch several buttons, equally spaced along fold, through all layers. With right sides facing and raw edges even, pin fringe to pillow front; stitch close to base of fringe. Pin front to back, with right sides facing and raw edges even; stitch together with $\frac{1}{2}$-inch seam, leaving 8-inch opening along one side. Clip corners, turn right side out, insert pillow form and slip-stitch opening closed.

Pleated Valance and Draperies

SKILL LEVEL: INTERMEDIATE

MATERIALS: $\frac{1}{2}$-inch-thick x 6-inch wide mounting board, cut 4 to 16 inches longer than outside window; tape measure; yardstick; pencil; handsaw; hand drill; 2 "L" brackets; large sheet of butcher paper; tailor's chalk; drapery fabric; coordinating cotton lining fabric; scissors; pins; matching thread; sewing machine; hand-sewing needle; iron and ironing board; coordinating flat braid trim; fabric or decorator's glue; staple gun and staples; mounting hardware; drapery rod, brackets and mounting hardware; curtain clips to fit rod

DIRECTIONS

1. For valance, measure, mark and cut the board to desired length. (Note: The ends of the board should extend from 2 to 8 inches on either side of the window frame depending on how much room is available and the fullness of your draperies. The more room you allow on either side of the window, the less of the window you'll cover when the draperies are pulled open.) Measure and mark desired placement of valance across window. Hold board in place at marks; mark placement of brackets on outside of window frame and underside of board about 2 to 4 inches from each end of board.

2. Remove board; drill starter screw guide holes in board and outside window frame at marks.

3. To make the pattern for the valance, cut a piece of butcher paper equal in length to the length of the mounting board, plus twice its width, plus 49 inches by a height equal to the desired length of the valance (about one-fifth the total window treatment height), plus $2\frac{1}{2}$ inches. Fold paper in half crosswise to mark center, then in quarters. Then divide each quarter into thirds, marking the pattern with lines at these points to divide the pattern into twelfths. Starting at one end, fold in a 4-inch-wide box pleat so that center of the pleat is at first mark (see Glossary on page 123 for instructions on how to fold a box pleat). (Note: If your fabric has a repeat, measure it, then determine how wide each of six box pleats needs to be to allow the pattern to be centered on the central scallop, and repeat evenly across the width of the valance. Multiply twice the width of each box pleat by six and add this measurement plus 1 inch to the pattern width. Be aware that the two box pleats near the ends of the valance will be centered on the corners of the mounting board.) Continue folding in box pleats at every odd twelfth mark. Pin pleats in place, then fold the paper into quarters again. Scale the scallop template (see page 109) to fit folded pattern, then trace scalloped edge onto one side of pattern, aligning bottom of scallop curve with center fold, and aligning top of scallop curve with quarter fold. Cut out pattern.

4. Cut two pieces of fabric to length of the unfolded pattern by its width at widest part, piecing fabric together and matching patterns at seams, if necessary, to achieve desired length.

5. Place the two pieces of fabric on top of each other, right sides facing. Pin opened pattern to fabric and cut fabric to pattern shape. Remove pattern.

6. With right sides facing and raw edges matching, sew the valance together with ½-inch seam, leaving the straight long edge open. Clip seam allowance along curve, turn right sides out and press.

7. Sew or glue trim to front scalloped edge of valance.

8. Fold fabric in half crosswise, right sides facing, and begin folding and pinning box pleats in place, as indicated on pattern, so that box pleats at ends are centered over corners of the mounting board. When pleats are pinned in place, position valance along mounting board to be sure outer pleats align with corners. If not, adjust pleats until they align properly. Press pleats.

9. Stitch along the top of the pleated fabric ½ inch from edge to secure pleats in place. Fold and press straight long edge toward back of valance 2 inches from edge.

10. Place 2-inch-wide folded edge along the top of the board. Starting at corners, staple the edge to the top of the board so the centers of the pleats at the ends align with the corners. Continue stapling about every 6 inches apart along length of the board. Wrap the ends of the valance around the board and staple in place.

11. Turn the board over and screw the brackets to the bottom of the board so that one leg of each L extends flush with the back edge of the board. Mount board to wall.

12. For draperies, mount drapery rod behind valance at desired height. Measure from top of rod to floor and add

7 inches or more, depending on how much you want your draperies to break at the floor (1 to 2 inches is standard). Measure the width of your window and add 4 inches. Measure, mark and cut two pieces from drapery fabric to these dimensions, piecing and matching patterns if necessary.

13. Measure from bottom of rod to floor. Measure outside width of window. Cut two pieces from lining fabric to these dimensions.

14. Fold and press a 1-inch double hem along the top of the drapery panels. Fold and press a 3-inch double hem along the bottom of the drapery panels. Blind-stitch to hem. Fold, press and stitch a 1-inch double hem along the lining panels.

15. With wrong sides facing, center lining panels over drapery panels, aligning raw top edge of lining with folded top hem of drapery. Fold over raw side edges of drapery fabric and pin to side edges of lining, sew lining to drapery fabric with ½-inch seams. Turn right side out, centering lining and pressing side hems so 1½ inches of drapery fabric folds over to lining side along each side edge.

16. Tuck raw top edges of lining under folded hems of drapery panels, and topstitch in place to secure hems. Evenly space clip rings along top edges of panel and thread onto rods.

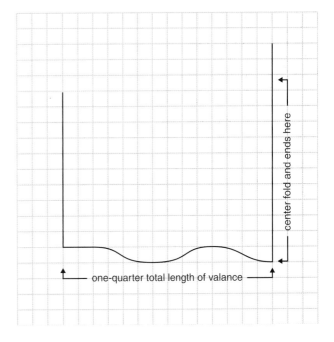

center fold and ends here

one-quarter total length of valance

Covered Chairs

SKILL LEVEL: BEGINNER

MATERIALS: Old upholstered chairs; hammer; staple remover; large sheet of butcher paper; pencil; upholstery fabric; pins; scissors; thick cotton batting; heavy-duty staple gun and staples; 1-inch brads or longer as may be needed

DIRECTIONS

1. Using claw end of hammer, remove any nails securing seat cushions and boards to chairs.

2. Remove staples securing fabric covers to boards. Remove fabric; smooth out and place on paper. Trace fabric shape onto paper to make pattern.

3. Fold paper pattern in half; redraw lines as needed to make pattern symmetrical.

4. Depending upon condition of padding on seat boards, add a layer or two of batting to existing padding. Cut batting ½ inch smaller all around than pattern. Center board, padded side down, on batting. Start in center of each side to staple batting to wrong side of board, working from front to back and side to side to keep batting taut and flat. Fold in excess at corners; staple in place.

5. Using pattern, cut fabric for each chair, centering fabric repeat if there is one. Place fabric facedown; center board, padded side down, on batting. Staple fabric in place in same manner as batting; before stapling corners, check front of cushion to make sure fabric is taut.

6. Place covered cushion back on chair; nail in place.

BARBARA'S DINING ROOM
Shaped Valance

SKILL LEVEL: INTERMEDIATE

MATERIALS: 3- to 6-inch-wide x ½-inch-thick mounting board; handsaw; decorator fabric; tape measure; yardstick; scissors; sewing machine and thread; beaded trim (optional); iron and ironing board; staple gun; level; drill and ⅛-inch drill bit; "L" metal brackets; ½- to ¾-inch screws; 1½- to 2-inch screws

DIRECTIONS

1. Measure window width from outside moldings. Cut mounting board so that it's 4 to 6 inches wider than the window width. Add twice the depth of the return—or the distance that the valance juts out from the wall— plus 1 inch for seam allowances plus length of mounting board. This will be the total width of the valance. (Note: Our mounting board was 3 inches deep, so total to cover the return on both ends was 6 inches.)

2. Measure the desired height of valance. The height of the valance should be one-fifth the height from the bottom of the window frame to the top of the valance. (Note: We mounted the valance 7 inches above the window, that distance was also added to the total window height figure.) Add 3 inches to this measurement for the header, or the portion of the valance that will be attached to the mounting board, plus ½ inch for the seam allowance. This will be the height of the valance.

3. Calculate the amount of fabric needed for each valance, by measuring the width of the fabric you have chosen for your project. If the width of the valance is less than the width of the fabric, you'll need only one length of fabric for each valance. Cut the lengths of fabric for the valance. If the valance is made up of more than one length of fabric, seam the lengths of fabric together, matching the pattern.

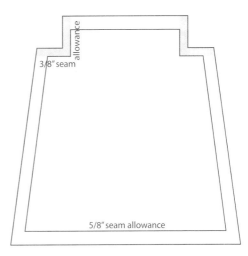

4. To create a shaped edge for the valance, cut a piece of pattern paper the width of the finished valance. For the valances shown, use the template (below) to create a pattern. Adjust the size and shape of the edge to suit the size of your valance. Place the pattern onto the fabric, and trace the lower edge with a fabric marking pen. Trim along the marked edge. (Note: If you're making more than one valance, it's important that the pattern repeat line up on each of the valances, so that each valance in the room looks the same. The easiest way to do this is to use the first panel to mark and cut each of the remaining valances. Place the completed panel over top of the next panel, and line up the pattern repeat. Mark and cut the next valance, and repeat for each of the valances needed.)

5. Mark and cut matching panels for the lining. For self-lined valances, match the fabric repeats just as you did for the valance face. Match the valance to the valance lining, right sides facing. If desired, add piping or trim at this time, sandwiching and pinning trim between valance and lining. Stitch across the lower edge of the valance. Trim and clip seam allowances. Understitch the seam.

6. Fold the seam allowances to the lining side, and stitch the side seams together. Turn the valance right side out. Press.

7. Clean-finish the top edge with a wide zigzag stitch, or serge the edge if you have an overlock machine available.

8. Press a 3-inch fold along the top edge of the valance, then center the valance along the mounting board and staple the 3-inch-wide edge to the top, folding crisply around returns. Using brackets, mount valance above window to wall. Repeat steps 4 through 8 for each of the valances.

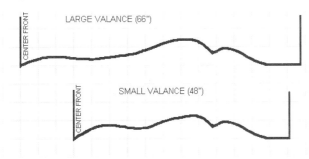

LARGE VALANCE (66")

SMALL VALANCE (48")

Tie-On Chair-Seat Covers

SKILL LEVEL: INTERMEDIATE

MATERIALS: Butcher paper; decorator fabric; tape measure; yardstick; scissors; pins; sewing machine and thread; muslin; drapery weight beads; iron and ironing board

DIRECTIONS

1. Use template (at right) to fit the Edvard chair we used from Ikea. If making a cover for your own chairs, use butcher paper to trace the chair seat. Add ⅝ inch around the outside edge for fitting ease and seam allowances. If the pattern has cutouts for the seat back, add ⅜ inch to the edge.

2. For skirt front, measure across the front of the chair and add 1 inch to this measurement for the seam allowances. For the pattern, cut a rectangle of pattern paper equal to this

measurement by 9 inches. Label the pattern Skirt Front.

3. For skirt sides, measure across the side of the chair, from the front edge to the leg and add 1 inch for seam allowances. For the pattern, cut a rectangle of pattern paper equal to this measurement by 9 inches. Label the pattern Skirt Side.

4. For skirt back, measure between the chair legs, and add 1 inch for seam allowances. Cut a rectangle of pattern paper equal to this measurement by 9 inches. Label the pattern Skirt Back.

5. Allow approximately 1 yard of fabric for each chair, and ½ yard of lining for every two chairs. This will vary depending on the size of the chair, and the pattern design of the fabric. The chair covers featured have a large floral design centered on each chair seat.

6. Place the chair seat pattern on the fabric, centering the design, pin in place. Cut out the first chair seat, and use it to match the pattern for each of the remaining seats. From the leftover fabric, pin patterns onto fabric and cut the chair skirts: one Skirt Front, one Skirt Back and two Skirt Sides for each chair. Cut four ties, 2½ x 16 inches. Pin chair seat pattern to lining fabric and cut a matching chair seat from the lining fabric for each chair.

7. Fold each tie lengthwise, and stitch across one short end and along the long side, using a ¼-inch seam. Turn right side out, and press.

8. Fold each front skirt lengthwise with right sides together. Sew the short ends with a ½-inch seam.

9. Pin a tie to each end of the Skirt Back, and fold lengthwise, enclosing the tie. Sew with a ½-inch seam.

10. Pin a tie to one end of each Skirt Side, and sew with a ½-inch seam. Turn the skirts right side out, and press. To keep the slipcover skirts from sticking out, consider using beaded drapery weights in the skirt.

11. Sew each skirt to the chair seat, using a ½-inch seam. With the chair skirts inside, match the chair seat to the lining. Sew the seat to the lining along the previous stitching line, leaving a 6-inch opening at the skirt back for turning right side out. Press.

12. Stitch "in the ditch" across the back skirt, sewing the opening closed.

JANE AND GREG'S KITCHEN
Layered Valance

SKILL LEVEL: BEGINNER

MATERIALS: ½-inch-thick x 6-inch-wide mounting board, cut 6 inches longer than outside window width; tape measure; pencil; handsaw; hand drill; 2 "L" brackets and mounting hardware; paint to match window frame; paintbrush; large sheet of butcher paper; yardstick; drapery fabric in two patterns or colors; chalk marking pencil; coordinating cotton lining fabric; coordinating fringe trim; coordinating piping; matching threads; scissors; pins; sewing machine; hand-sewing needle; iron and ironing board; self-adhesive hook-and-loop fastener tape

DIRECTIONS

1. Measure and mark the desired placement of the valance across window. Hold the board in place at the marks; mark the placement of the brackets on the wall outside of the window frame and under the board.

2. Remove the board; drill screw guide holes in the board and into the wall at the marks.

3. Mount the board over window frame, using a bracket on each end.

4. Paint the board and let it dry.

5. To make the pattern for the valance, cut the paper so that its width equals the window width plus 12 inches and its height is equal to the measurement from the top of the valance to the deepest part of the valance, plus 1 inch all around. (Note: The height of the valance should be about one-fifth the height from the top of the mounting board to the bottom of the windowsill.) Freehand-draw the desired valance shape on paper, adjusting to fit the size of your window. Draw an additional line ½ inch below the desired shape; cut out the pattern. Fold the pattern in half; trim as needed so valance is symmetrical.

6. Open the pattern and pin it to the underlayer of fabric and cut it out. Then pin it to the lining fabric and cut it out. Cut off 5 inches from the top of the valance pattern to make

Trimmed Chandelier Lampshades

SKILL LEVEL: BEGINNER

MATERIALS: Chandelier; lampshade kits in desired size, with chandelier clips; fabric as desired; scissors; narrow braid or trim as desired; hot-glue gun and glue sticks

DIRECTIONS

1. For each lampshade, cut fabric to same size as adhesive lampshade cover from kit; if shade has a protective paper covering, use that as a pattern. Following kit manufacturer's directions, remove paper backing and press fabric onto cover, smoothing from center out to eliminate air bubbles.

2. Cut braid to fit along lower edge of lampshade; glue in place, butting raw ends.

3. Place shades over chandelier bulbs; clip in place.

a new pattern for the overlayer of the valance. Pin the pattern to the overlayer of fabric and cut it out. Then pin it to the lining fabric and cut it out.

7. Pin piping to the lower and side edges of checked fabric, with right sides facing and base of piping ½ inch from fabric edges. Using a zipper foot, baste close to the base of the piping.

8. With right sides facing and raw edges even, pin each valance to its matching lining. Stitch along the raw edges with a ½-inch seam, leaving an opening along the upper edge. Trim the corners and clip the seams. Turn the valances right side out; press. Slip-stitch the openings closed to make each layer.

9. With overlayer of valance faceup, pin the fringe along the lower edge so it overlaps valance by ½ inch, turning under the fringe at the ends. Stitch close to upper edge of fringe.

10. With right sides up, and upper edges even, place the overlayer of valance on top of the underlayer. Baste the upper edges together to create one valance.

11. Cut the hook-and-loop tape to fit front and sides of valance board. Peel off the backing; adhere the hook side to board and the loop side to the upper edge of valance. Press the two halves of the hook-and-loop tape together to secure the valance in place; remove tape for laundering.

SUSAN AND ANDY'S KITCHEN
Roman Shades

SKILL LEVEL: INTERMEDIATE

MATERIALS: 1-inch-wide x ½-inch-thick mounting board (Note: Width of board should be about ¼ inch shorter than the depth of window frame and length of board should be about ⅛ inch shorter than inside width of window frame); yardstick; pencil; handsaw; plaid fabric (or fabric of your choice); lining fabric; chalk marking pencil; tape measure; pins; scissors; matching threads; sewing machine; 1½-inch-wide coordinating grosgrain ribbon; hand-sewing needle; ½-inch plastic rings; heavy-duty staple gun and staples; 2 screw eyes; cord; hand drill with drill and screwdriver bits; 1½- to 2-inch wood screws; cord pull; awning cleat and mounting hardware

DIRECTIONS

1. Measure, mark and cut the mounting board.

2. For shade, measure inside window width and length; add 1 inch to each measurement. Cut a piece of fabric and lining to these dimensions. For valance, divide window length by five, add width of mounting board plus 1 inch. Measure, mark and cut a piece of fabric and lining to this measurement by the inside width of the window.

3. Pin shade to lining, with right sides facing and raw edges even. Stitch edges with ½-inch seam, leaving top edge open. Turn right side out; press. Repeat for valance.

4. With right sides up, pin ribbon about 1 inch from side and lower edges of shade, folding to miter ribbon at corners. Pin ribbon about 1 inch from side and lower edges of

valance in same manner. Stitch close to all edges of ribbon.

5. Pin top edge of valance to top edge of shade, with right sides of each facing up. Sew together with ½-inch seam.

6. With wrong side up, mark ring placement on back of shade. Place first rings 3 inches from each side edge and 4 inches from bottom edge. Depending on width of your window, you may also want to add one or more rows of additional rings, equally spaced about 8 to 10 inches apart between the first two rings. Hand-stitch rings to lining and shade.

7. Above the first set of rings, continue marking positions of rings in horizontal rows. Each row should be about 8 inches apart and the last one should end about 6 inches below top seam. Sew rings to lining and shade.

8. Align upper edge of wrong side of shade with upper back edge of wide side of mounting board; staple in place.

9. Mark placement of screw eyes on underside of board, directly above each vertical row of rings. Use drill to make small pilot holes; screw eyes in place.

10. Cut a piece of cord for each vertical row, each two and a half times the length of window. Tie a cord to bottom ring on each vertical row. String cord up through each ring in each row, then through screw eye above. Decide whether cords will hang on left or right side of window, then string cord or cords through screw eye or eyes toward the one on cord side, so all cords go through screw eye and hang on one side of shade.

11. Measure and mark positions of screws on mounting board, starting about 2 inches from each side edge and equally spacing between screw eyes. Fold raw edge of ½-inch seam toward top of board, then screw board into top of window so self-valance hangs in front. With shade lowered, adjust cord length so tension is equal on all cords, thread cords through pull, then knot cords together about three-quarters of the way down shade. Trim excess cord below knot.

12. Screw cleat to wall about halfway down window length; pull cords to raise shade to desired level, then wrap them around cleat to secure shade.

SHAR'S KITCHEN
Banquette Seating

SKILL LEVEL: INTERMEDIATE

MATERIALS: Tape measure; utility knife ; 3-inch-thick foam cushions; heavy foam pillow forms in desired size for backs; cotton fabrics in desired prints; matching thread; 1-inch-wide curtain shirring tape; narrow cotton cord for piping; scissors; pins; sewing machine; hand-sewing needle; chalk marking pencil; self-adhesive hook-and-loop fastener tape

NOTE: All stitching is done with ½-inch seams, right sides facing and raw edges even, unless otherwise specified.

DIRECTIONS

1. Measure, mark and cut the seat cushion foam to fit the seats. For the seat covers, measure the length and width of the cushions; add 4 inches to each measurement. Cut two pieces of fabric to these measurements for each cushion for the top and bottom.

2. Cut the remaining fabric into 2-inch-wide bias strips; stitch strips together end to end to make a long cover strip for the piping.

3. To make the piping, fold the strip lengthwise over the cord, right side out; stitch close to the base of the cord, using a zipper foot. Set the piping aside.

4. For the cushion top, fold in one corner of the fabric toward wrong side of fabric on the diagonal about 2 inches

from the corner; and finger-press the fold. Mark a line perpendicular to the fold from the corner point to the fold; right sides facing, fold each side of the finger-pressed fold to align with the marked line and pin in place. Stitch along the line through both layers to form mitered boxed corner. Miter each corner of the cushion top in the same manner. Miter each corner of the cushion bottom in the same manner. Trim the excess fabric at the corners.

5. Pin the piping to edge of the top; stitch close to the base of the piping.

6. Pin the cushion top to the cushion bottom; start near the end of one long side to stitch along all edges, stopping near the other end of the same long side, leaving this side with a large opening. Turn fabric right side out; insert the cushion. Slip-stitch the opening closed.

7. For the back pillow covers, measure the length and width of the pillows; add 1 inch to each measurement. Cut two pieces of fabric to these measurements for each pillow for the front and back for the cover.

8. Make piping as described for the seat covers (see steps 2 and 3).

9. Pin the piping to edge of the right side of the top, raw edges matching; stitch close to the base of the piping, using a zipper foot.

10. Pin the front to the back; stitch, leaving a 10-inch opening along one long side. Turn the cover right side out; insert the pillow form. Slip-stitch the opening closed.

11. For the seat ruffle, measure the length of the banquette, including all sides that will have a ruffle; multiply this measurement by two and a half. For the ruffle height, measure the desired height and add 4 inches. Cut the fabric to these measurements, piecing as needed.

12. On each short end of the ruffle, turn under 1 inch, then 1 inch again. Stitch close to the folds to hem the ends.

13. Hem one long edge of the ruffle in the same manner.

14. On remaining edge (which will be the upper edge), turn under ½ inch, then 1½ inches; stitch close to the fold.

15. Cut curtain tape to the same length as the upper edge; pin the tape to the wrong side of the ruffle, with the upper edges even. Stitch close to both long edges of the tape.

16. Pull up the tape cords so the ruffle is same length as the banquette edge; knot the cords to secure.

17. Cut the hook-and-loop tape to this length; peel off the backing and attach the hook side to the ruffle, over the curtain tape, and the loop side to edge of banquette. Press the ruffle into place on the banquette edge.

Barstool Covers

SKILL LEVEL: INTERMEDIATE

MATERIALS: Large sheet of butcher paper; pencil; pins; cotton fabrics: 1 yard of main color, $\frac{1}{4}$ yard of contrasting color for each barstool; scissors; tape measure; 2 yards coordinating piping for each barstool; matching threads; sewing machine

NOTE: All stitching is done with $\frac{1}{2}$-inch seams, right sides facing and raw edges even, unless otherwise specified.

DIRECTIONS

1. Trace the top of the stool on the butcher paper using the pencil. Add $\frac{1}{2}$ inch all around to make the top pattern. Pin the pattern to the main fabric and cut it out.

2. Measure the perimeter of the seat and triple this measurement. Cut a piece of the main fabric to this length by 8 inches deep, piecing as needed, for the ruffled skirt. Add 1 inch to the seat perimeter measurement; measure the height of seat and add 1 inch. Cut a strip of contrasting fabric to these measurements.

3. Pin the short ends of the ruffle together; stitch to form a ring.

4. Turn under $\frac{1}{2}$ inch, then $\frac{3}{4}$ inch, along one edge of the ruffle; press. Stitch close to fold to hem ruffle.

5. Using long machine basting stitches, stitch $\frac{1}{2}$ inch, then $\frac{1}{4}$ inch, from raw edge of ruffle, beginning and ending at the seam. Pull up the thread ends to gather the ruffle.

6. With raw edges even, pin the piping along each long edge of contrasting strip. Machine-baste close to the base of the piping, using a zipper foot. Pin and stitch short the ends of the contrasting strip together to form a ring.

7. Pin and stitch one edge of the contrasting ring to the gathered edge of the ruffle, pulling up the threads to gather the ruffle evenly. Pin and stitch one edge of the ring to the circular top fabric; clip the curves.

Trimmed Gingham Bedskirt

SKILL LEVEL: INTERMEDIATE

MATERIALS: King-size flat cotton sheet; tape measure; yardstick; tailor's chalk; scissors; iron and ironing board; medium-weight black-and-white cotton gingham fabric; matching thread; pins; sewing machine; $1\frac{1}{2}$-inch-wide black grosgrain ribbon

DIRECTIONS

1. Measure length and width of bed; add 1 inch to each measurement. Measure, mark and cut flat sheet to these measurements for skirt base. Along one short end of base (for head of bed), turn under $\frac{1}{4}$ inch, then $\frac{1}{4}$ inch again and press; to hem base, stitch close to fold.

2. Double the bed length measurement; add bed width measurement plus 40 inches. Measure from top of box spring to floor; add $2\frac{1}{2}$ inches. Cut gingham to these measurements, piecing as needed.

3. Turn under 1 inch, then 1 inch again, on each short end of skirt and press; stitch close to folds to hem side edges of skirt. Hem one long edge (lower edge) of skirt in same manner.

4. Pin ribbon to right side of skirt, about 5 inches above lower hem. Stitch ribbon to skirt along both edges, turning under ends at side ends of skirt.

5. With right sides facing and raw edges even, begin pinning skirt to base where short hemmed ends of skirt align with hemmed edge of base. At each lower corner where skirt wraps along the foot end of base, form a box pleat in skirt (see Glossary on page 123 for instructions on how to make box pleats). At center of foot edge of base, form a box pleat in skirt with remaining excess fabric so skirt fabric lies flat and pin in place. Stitch all edges with $\frac{1}{2}$-inch seam; clip corners.

6. Remove mattress; place base on box spring so skirt hangs evenly on all sides. Place mattress back on box spring.

ANN'S MASTER BEDROOM
Bullion-Fringed Bedskirt

SKILL LEVEL: INTERMEDIATE

MATERIALS: King-size flat cotton sheet; tape measure; yardstick; tailor's chalk; scissors; iron and ironing board; pins; sewing machine; cream-colored cotton medium-weight fabric; matching bullion fringe, about 4 inches long; matching thread

DIRECTIONS

1. Measure width and length of bed; add 1 inch to each measurement. Measure, mark and cut a flat sheet to these measurements for skirt base. Along one short end of base (for head of bed), turn under ¼ inch, then ¼ inch again and press; stitch close to fold to hem.

2. Double the bed length measurement then add bed width measurement plus 40 inches. Measure from top of box spring to floor. Cut cotton fabric to these measurements for skirt, piecing as needed.

3. Turn under 1 inch, then 1 inch again, on each short end of skirt and press; stitch close to folds to hem side edges of skirt. Hem one long edge (lower edge) of skirt in same manner.

4. With right sides facing and raw edges even, begin pinning skirt to base where short hemmed ends of skirt align with hemmed edge of base. At each lower corner where skirt wraps along the foot end of base, form a box pleat in skirt (see Glossary on page 123 for instructions on how to make box pleats). At center of foot edge of base, form a box pleat in skirt with remaining excess fabric so skirt fabric lies flat and pin in place. Stitch all edges with ½-inch seam; clip corners.

5. With right sides up, pin fringe close to lower edge of skirt. Overlap edges so fringe is about ½ inch above floor (hold skirt up to bed to test length). Stitch close to upper edge of fringe through all layers.

6. Remove mattress; place base on box spring so skirt hangs evenly on all sides. Place mattress back on box spring.

Antiqued Side Table

SKILL LEVEL: INTERMEDIATE

MATERIALS: Old wooden side table or chest; screwdriver; gel paint stripper; paintbrushes; rubber gloves; soft cotton cloths; wire furniture-stripping brush; paint primer; paintbrushes; acrylic paints in ivory and brown; painter's glaze mix; mixing pans; natural sponges; polyurethane sealer; metal drawer pulls; black spray paint

DIRECTIONS

1. Remove drawers from table and drawer pulls from drawers. Wearing rubber gloves, coat drawers and table with stripper; allow to set, following manufacturer's directions, then wipe off excess. Use wire brush to remove stripper and paint from carved areas of wood. Reapply stripper to these areas if needed. Wipe stripped wood with soft cloths to remove all residue.

2. Apply primer to all surfaces of wood; let dry.

3. Apply two coats of ivory-colored paint to drawer fronts and table, letting dry after each coat.

4. To make brown wash, mix some brown paint with small amount of glaze. Using sponge, lightly apply strokes along top of table; let dry.

5. To glaze table, add more glaze to paint/glaze mixture; test mixture on inconspicuous area to make sure it's sheer enough. Brush a light coat of glaze on drawer fronts and table; while glaze is still wet, use sponge to remove excess, allowing glaze to remain darkest in carved areas of wood. Let dry. Apply additional coats of glaze as desired for antique effect, letting dry after each coat.

6. Apply two coats of polyurethane sealer to drawer fronts and table, letting dry after each coat.

7. Spray drawer pulls black, applying several light coats to prevent drips. Let dry after each coat.

8. Attach pulls to drawers; place drawers back in table.

LEAH'S BEDROOM
Bamboo Headboard

SKILL LEVEL: BEGINNER

MATERIALS: 30 x 60-inch bordered bamboo mat;
3 to 5 metal or plastic rings; thread; hand-sewing needle;
heavy-duty scissors; carpenter's level; pencil; hammer;
3 to 5 picture hooks and nails

DIRECTIONS

1. On the back of the mat, mark the placement of the rings along one long edge at both ends and equally spaced along the top border.

2. Hand-sew the rings at the marks, making sure they're hidden by the border when viewed from the front.

3. Hold the headboard against the wall to mark placement above bed; mark upper and side edges of headboard lightly on wall, using a carpenter's level to make sure the top is straight.

4. Measure and mark the placement of the picture hooks.

5. Hammer the hooks into the wall at the marks; hang the headboard on the hooks.

Asian Curtain Rod

SKILL LEVEL: BEGINNER

MATERIALS: 3 bamboo garden stakes, about ½ inch in diameter; tape measure; pencil; utility knife; jute or hemp twine; scissors; 2 rod brackets and mounting hardware; hand drill with drill and screwdriver bits; yardstick; pencil

DIRECTIONS

1. Measure, mark and cut each stake, using the utility knife, so that they're about 8 inches longer than the width of your window. Holding the stakes in a bundle, wrap and tie twine about 3 inches from each end. For very wide windows, wrap and tie additional twine around the center as well.

2. Measure and mark the placement of rod above window. Hold the brackets in place as desired to mark the screw placement.

3. Drill a small screw pilot hole at each mark. Screw the brackets to wall at marks. Place the curtain on the rod and place the rod on the brackets.

Glass Vase Lamp

SKILL LEVEL: BEGINNER

MATERIALS: Make-a-Lamp kit (available at crafts stores); glass vase or bottle; drill and ceramic drill bit (optional); lampshade; hardware and tools as required for lamp kit

NOTE: Make sure your shade is properly proportioned for your vase.

DIRECTIONS

1. Wash and dry the vase. Follow the lamp kit directions to prepare the vase for wiring (some kits require holes to be drilled; use a hand drill with a ceramic bit for making holes in ceramic or glass).

2. Insert the wiring through the vase, hooking the shade clips onto the top of the vase so the lamp socket is centered on the vase.

3. Clip the shade onto the lamp.

SUSAN AND ANDY'S BEDROOM
Hinged Fire Screen

SKILL LEVEL: BEGINNER

MATERIALS: Yardstick; pencil; ½-inch-thick plywood; handsaw or circular saw (optional); sandpaper; tack cloth; 2-inch-wide lattice or 12 picture stretchers (6 should measure the height of the screen; 4 should be the width of the two side panels; 2 the width of the center panel); primer; paintbrushes; wood glue; hammer and ½- or ¾-inch brads; painter's tape; latex paint; miter box and saw (optional); screwdriver; hinges

DIRECTIONS

1. Measure the height and width of your fireplace opening. Measure, mark and cut three panels from the plywood, with the center panel measuring 1 inch higher than the opening and about two-thirds the width, and the two side panels measuring 1 inch higher than the opening and about one-quarter the width. (Note: You can bring your measurements with you to the lumber store, and an employee can usually precut the wood for you if you prefer.)

2. Prime both sides and edges of the lumber, letting one side dry completely, before priming the other. After priming, let the other side dry. Sand the smooth side of the wood to remove any flaws, wipe off dust with a tack cloth.

3. Fit together picture stretchers to form molding for each panel and nail in place. Or cut lattice, mitered at corners, to create molding around panels instead. Glue and nail in place.

4. Apply painter's tape to each panel in pattern shown in photograph. Apply two coats of paint to panels, letting dry between coats. Remove tape. Join panels with hinges so both side panels fold away from front.

Monogrammed Pillow

SKILL LEVEL: INTERMEDIATE

MATERIALS: Yardstick; tailor's chalk or pencil; ½ yard solid decorator-weight fabric; contrasting cotton fabric for welting; scissors; 2¼ yards of ¼-inch cotton cording; tweezers; iron and ironing board; pins; sewing machine with

embroidery capability; all-purpose thread; embroidery hoop; tear-away stabilizer; embroidery design (4-inch monogram letter); machine embroidery thread; 12 x 16-inch pillow form; 6 1-inch buttons

DIRECTIONS

1. Measure, mark and cut decorator fabric into one 8 x 12-inch center panel, two 5 x 12-inch side panels, and two 10 x 12-inch back panels. Measure, mark and cut the contrasting fabric into two 1¾ x 45-inch strips.

2. To create the monogram, set the program for your design, place the 8 x 12-inch center fabric in a medium-sized embroidery hoop along with a piece of tear-away stabilizer underneath it. Embroider the 4-inch monogram in the center of the fabric using the embroidery thread. Remove the stabilizer.

3. To create welting, join the two 1¾ x 45-inch strips together by overlapping the ends of the strip. With right sides together, place one end 90 degrees against the other. Stitch a seam from one edge to the opposite edge. Trim seam to ¼ inch.

4. To sew the welting, fold the fabric strip, wrong sides together, encasing the cording and matching raw edges. Using a slightly longer than normal stitch length and a zipper foot, stitch close to the cording. Cut two pieces of cording equal to the length of the sides of the center panel. Using the zipper foot, attach cording to both sides of monogrammed center panel, matching raw edges and stitching over the previous stitching. To eliminate bulk at the edges, use a tweezers to carefully pull out about ½ inch of the cording and trim it away. Ease the cording back into the casing.

5. With right sides facing, sew the two side panels to the welted edges of the center panel. Press the seams toward the center panel. Sew three buttons on each side panel.

6. Using a zipper foot, sew welting around perimeter edges of pillow front, clipping cording seam allowances at corners.

7. Narrowly hem one long edge of each of the 10 x 12-inch back pieces. Overlap the hemmed edges so that when together, they measure 16 inches across. With wrong sides together, pin the pillow front to the pillow back. Using the zipper foot, sew the pillow together stitching close to the cording. Turn cover right side out. Insert the pillow form.

Shaped Headboard

SKILL LEVEL: ADVANCED

MATERIALS: Butcher paper; yardstick; pencil; tape measure; fabric; scissors; ¼-inch cording; all-purpose thread; ½-inch-thick plywood; jigsaw; 2 x 4 lumber (optional); circular saw (optional); hammer and nails (optional); rolls of 2-inch-thick foam; batting; staple gun; drill and drill bit (optional); awl (optional); 3-inch bolts and nuts (optional)

DIRECTIONS

1. Determine the desired height of your headboard—we chose to make ours 5 feet tall. Using the template (below), enlarge it to scale and draw the headboard shape onto butcher paper to make a pattern, extending sides so that the center of the headboard meets your desired height. Add ½ inch all around for seam allowance.

2. Calculate the yardage necessary to make a two-sided slipcover, plus gusset and self-welting. To determine the length of fabric needed to create the side gusset, measure along the sides and top of the headboard pattern. The width of the gusset should equal the thickness of the headboard foam—ours was 2 inches—plus 1 inch for the seam allowances. Cut enough strips of fabric so that, when joined together with ½-inch seam allowances, they equal the required gusset length.

3. The welting strips need to be twice the length of the gusset, as the welting is applied to both sides of the headboard. Cut enough 1¾-inch-wide strips on the bias so that, when joined together with ½-inch seam allowances, they equal the required length of welting. To join the welting strips together, overlap the ends of the strips with right sides facing, placing one end 90 degrees against the other. Stitch a seam diagonally from one edge to the opposite edge. Trim seams to ¼ inch.

4. To create the welting, fold the completed fabric strip around the cording, wrong sides together, matching raw edges. Using a slightly longer than normal stitch length and a zipper foot, stitch close to the cording.

5. A queen- or king-size headboard is most likely wider than the width of your fabric. If so, use one width of the fabric for the center panel and add two panels of fabric on either side. Sew the side panels to the center panel, matching the pattern, if necessary. Pin the headboard pattern to the

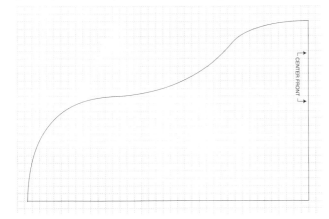

seamed fabric and cut the fabric along the pattern. Repeat for the other side of the headboard.

6. Use a zipper foot to stitch the cording along the shaped edges of each of the headboard pieces. Stitch over previous stitching, clipping cording seam allowances at curves and corners.

7. Sew one long edge of the side gusset strip to the welted edge of one of the headboard pieces. Sew the opposite edge of the side gusset strip to the welted edge of the other headboard piece. Finish the bottom edge with a narrow double hem.

8. Use the template to trace the headboard shape onto the plywood. Using a jigsaw, cut out the headboard form. Plywood comes in 4 x 8-foot sheets, so if your headboard will be taller than 4 feet, you'll need to build up the height by adding 2- to 3-foot-long extensions of 2 x 4 lumber. Using a jigsaw or a circular saw, cut three 2 x 4 extensions to the length you require. Nail the extensions to the plywood form, allowing a foot or more to extend beyond the base of the plywood form on both sides and in center.

9. Use the template to mark the shape of the headboard on the 2-inch-thick foam, and cut out the shape with scissors or utility knife. Apply spray glue to the plywood form on the side with the attached extensions, if you have them, and position the cut piece of foam on the form, aligning the shaped edges. Cut another piece of foam equal to the width of the headboard, and place it beneath the first piece of foam on the form across the width of the form. Drape batting over the foam, wrapping it around to the back of the form and securing it in place with a staple gun. If your bed frame has fittings to secure the headboard to the frame, measure and mark the positions for holes on the plywood or lumber extensions and drill holes in these spots.

10. Slip headboard cover over the padded headboard form. Lean headboard against wall and slide bed up against it in place. If you want to bolt the headboard to fittings on your bed frame, using the awl, poke holes through the fabric in alignment with drilled holes, bolts through all layers and secure with nuts.

GLOSSARY

BIAS STRIPS: Strips of fabric cut diagonally to the straight grain of the fabric.

BLIND STITCH: Sewing stitch that is not meant to be seen on the right side of the fabric, usually accomplished by picking up one thread of the fabric at a time rather than going through the full fabric or several threads before completing a hand stitch or machine stitch. Many sewing machines come with a blind hem attachment and the manual is the best guide for how to use it and produce virtually invisible hems.

BOX PLEAT: A double pleat having two upper folds facing in opposite directions and two under folds pressed toward each other. To make a box pleat, determine the width of the finished pleat, fold the fabric, right sides facing, along the center point of the pleat, pin the fabric together along the upper edge at a point that's twice the width of the finished pleat, align the center point of the pleat with the point where the fabric is pinned, press the newly folded edges to form the box pleat and baste in place.

BRAD: A thin, short finishing nail with a small diameter head and shank of no longer than 1½ inches.

BUTCHER PAPER: A roll of white paper in various lengths available at art supply and crafts stores.

DECORATOR FABRIC: Upholstery- or drapery-weight printed or woven fabric.

GLAZE: A translucent layer of paint through which other layers of paint can be seen.

JABOT: The cascading fabric at each side of a swag or valance.

MITER BOX: Hand tool for guiding handsaws in making crosscuts or miter joints.

PATTERN REPEAT: The interval between the repetition of the same pattern.

PICTURE WIRE: Braided wire for supporting framed pictures. Choose one rated to have at least four times the breaking strength of the weight of your framed picture.

SCREW EYE: A woodscrew having its shank bent into a ring.

SLIP STITCH: Loose stitch catching only a thread or two of fabric; designed to be invisible from the right side.

TAILOR'S CHALK: Chalk used by tailors to make temporary marks on cloth.

VALANCE: An ornamental drapery treatment, usually made of fabric, typically no longer that 20 inches in numerous styles.

WHIPSTITCH: A stitch passing over an edge diagonally.

ZIPPER FOOT: A specialty sewing machine foot that enables you to sew a line of stitches close to the edge of a zipper or encased piping.

PRODUCT INFORMATION

ANN'S FAMILY ROOM: Window treatment and slipcover, Linda Grimm Designs; wall paint, Manila, Ralph Lauren Home; armoire, Broyhill; couches, Mitchell Gold; tables, ottoman, Home Elements.

JANE AND GREG'S FAMILY ROOM: Sofa slipcover, large Classic Piped Twill in Light Stone, chair slipcover, medium Classic Twill T-cushion, in Light Stone, all Lands' End.

SUSAN AND ANDY'S FAMILY ROOM: Shades fabric, Harvest Stripe, tailored square pillows in Canvas Sage with Moss cording, wooden blinds, 2-inch with twill tapes, all Smith+Noble.

PETER'S LIVING ROOM: Sofa slipcover and plaid throw, Lands' End; chair slipcover, Sure Fit; Quick Shades, Levelor/Kirsch.

JUDY AND BOB'S LIVING ROOM: Furniture and accessories, all Big Lots; draperies, Pottery Barn; wicker chair cushion fabric, Waverly.

JANE'S DINING ROOM: Window treatment fabric, Calico Corners.

SUSAN AND ANDY'S DINING ROOM: Window treatment fabric and trim, chair fabric, all Robert Allen.

BARBARA'S DINING ROOM: Valance fabric, Hope chest stripe, chair seat cover fabric, Forever yours, in Spring, all Waverly; dining chairs, Edvard, white, Ikea; rug, Egeby, sisal, Ikea; cabinet, Country Stand, Woodcraft Industries; furniture paint, Butter, Benjamin Moore.

JANE'S KITCHEN: Wall paint, Citrus Green, Benjamin Moore; window treatment fabric, Calico Corners; trivet, pant stand, bowls, vase, Southern Living at Home; backsplash wallcovering, Duncan Wallcoverings & Paint; slipcovers, Lands' End; table and chairs, bare Wood Furniture.

SUSAN AND ANDY'S KITCHEN: window treatment fabric, Blair House Check, blue, American spirit Collection, Waverly; trim, 1½-inch-wide grosgrain, C.M. Offray & Sons.

SHAR'S KITCHEN: Sink, Kohler; faucet, Pegasus; cabinet hardware, Pottery Barn; backsplash tile, American Olean; paint, Sherwin-Williams.

ANN'S GUEST BEDROOMS: Finials, Pottery Barn; wall paint, Pale Almond, Benjamin Moore; end tables, Home Goods; flooring, sisal rug, Ballard; bed, chairs, Pottery Barn.

ANN'S MASTER BEDROOM: Window treatments, Linens 'n Things.

LEAH'S BEDROOM: Wall paint, Reflecting Pool, Glidden; headboard, 30×60-inch mat, bedspread, bottle (for lamp base), dot box, all Home Goods; Make-A-Lamp kit, bamboo rods, hollowcore doors (for screen), all Home Depot; curtains, bamboo roll-up blind, table, Ikea; frames, Timeless Frames; pillows; slipcover, Hampton Check, Sure Fit; mirror frame spray paint, Chrome, Krylon; wallpaper (on screen), Gramercy.

SUSAN AND ANDY'S BEDROOM: Window treatment fabric, Lightfoot House, window treatment border fabric, Henderson, slipcover fabric, Ballroom Plaid, headboard fabric, Bryan House Trellis, all Waverly; all soft goods, sewn on Singer sewing machine, The Singer Company; wall paint, armoire paint, night-stands and fire screen paint, all Benjamin Moore; nightstands, Woodcraft Industries; bedding, The Company Store; headboard foam, batting, Fairfield Processing; needlepoint pillow and clock, Gracious Home; footed bowl, glass pitcher, Crate & Barrel; pillowcases, woven tray, Target; embroidered pillow, Milli Home; entertainment armoire, Woodcraft Industries.

SHAR'S BATHROOM: Contractor, David Cipriano, Cipriano Construction Co.; designer, Shar Cipriano, Reflections of You; carpenter, Steve Brouner Carpentry; plumber, Carey Ritmiller, Rhino Plumbing; tub, Montrose, in white, Lasco Bathware; sinks and toilet, Kohler; wall tiles, American Olean; flooring, Dal-Tile; sink fittings, Delta; lighting, chrome sconces, Hampton Bay; windows, Jeld-Wen; shutters, Shutters Northwest, Inc.; wall paint, Sherwin-Williams; "Wash" sign, Pottery Barn; curtains, Target; accessories (on vanity), Bed Bath & Beyond.

SOURCES

C.M. OFFRAY & SONS
RIBBONS
(800) 344-5533
www.offray.com

AMERICAN OLEAN
TILES
www.americanolean.com

BALLARD DESIGN
FURNITURE
(800) 367-2810
www.ballardesign.com

BED, BATH AND BEYOND
HOME PRODUCTS
(800) 462-3966
www.bedbathandbeyond.com

BENJAMIN MOORE
PAINT
(800) 304-0304
www.benjaminmoore.com

BERH
PAINT
(800) 462-3966
www.behr.com

BIG LOTS
HOUSEHOLD PRODUCTS
www.biglots.com

BROYHILL
FURNITURE
(800) 327-6944
www.broyhillfurn.com

CALICO CORNERS
FABRICS, TRIMMINGS, CUSTOM
PRODUCTS
(800) 213-6366
www.calicocorners.com

THE COMPANY STORE
HOME PRODUCTS, BEDDING, BATH
(800) 323-8000
www.thecompanystore.com

CRATE & BARREL
HOME PRODUCTS
(800) 967-6696
www.crateandbarrel.com

DAL-TILE
TILES
(214) 398-1411
www.daltile.com

DELTA
BATHROOM FIXTURES
(800) 345-3358
deltacom.deltafaucet.com

**DUNCAN WALLCOVERINGS
& PAINT**
WALLCOVERING, PAINT
(502) 896-4441

FAIRFIELD PROCESSING CORP.
SEWING AND CRAFTS MATERIAL
(800) 980-8000
www.poly-fil.com

GLIDDEN
PAINT
(800) 454-3336
www.gliddenpaint.com

GRACIOUS HOME
HOME PRODUCTS
(212) 231-7800
www.gracioushome.com

GRAMERCY WALLPAPER
WALLPAPER, FABRIC
www.fschumacher.com

THE HOME DEPOT
HOME IMPROVEMENT RETAILER
(800) 553-3199
www.homedepot.com

HOME ELEMENTS
FURNITURE
(905) 985-8234
www.settlementhouse.com

HOME GOODS
HOME PRODUCTS
(800) 614-4663

IKEA
HOME PRODUCTS
(800) 434-4532
www.ikea-usa.com

JELD-WEN
WINDOWS AND DOORS
(877)-535-3462
www.jeld-wen.com

KOHLER
PLUMBING PRODUCTS
(800) 456-4536
www.kohlerco.com

KRYLON
PAINT
(800) 4KRYLON
www.krylon.com

LANDS' END
HOME PRODUCTS
(800) 356-4444
www.landsend.com

LASCO BATHWARE
BATH FIXTURES
www.lascobathware.com

LEVELOR
SHADES AND BLINDS
(800) 538-6567
www.levelor.com

LINDA GRIMM DESIGNS
WINDOW TREATMENTS
(217) 498-7869

LINENS 'N THINGS
HOME PRODUCTS
(866) 568-7378
www.lnt.com

MILLI HOME
HOME TEXTILES
(212) 643-8850
www.millihome.com

MITCHELL GOLD
FURNITURE
www.mitchellgold.com

PEGASUS
PLUMBING PRODUCTS
(888) 328-2383
www.pegasusfaucets.com

POSH ROOMS
INTERIOR DESIGN
(703) 726-0058
poshrooms@aol.com

POTTERY BARN
HOME PRODUCTS
(888) 779-5176
www.potterybarn.com

RALPH LAUREN HOME
HOME PRODUCTS
(888) 475-7674
www.rlhome.polo.com

REFLECTIONS OF YOU
INTERIOR DESIGN
(503) 667-9755

ROBERT ALLEN
TEXTILE DESIGN
(800) 333-3777
www.robertallendesign.com

SHERWIN-WILLIAMS
PAINT
www.sherwin-williams.com

SHUTTERS NORTHWEST
BLINDS
(800) 886-4635
www.shuttersnw.com

THE SINGER COMPANY
SEWING MACHINES
(800) 4-SINGER
www.singerco.com

SMITH+NOBLE
WINDOW TREATMENTS
(800) 506-0027
www.smithandnoble.com

SOUTHERN LIVING AT HOME
HOME PRODUCTS
www.southernlivingathome.com

SURE FIT
SLIPCOVERS, FABRICS
(800) 305-5857
www.surefit.com

TARGET
HOME PRODUCTS
(800) 440-0680
www.target.com

TIMELESS FRAMES
FRAMES
(800) 945-0431
www.timelessframes.com

WAVERLY
WALLPAPER AND FABRIC
(800) 423-5881
www.waverly.com

WOODCRAFT INDUSTRIES
FURNITURE
www.woodcraftindustries.com

CREDITS

pp. 12–15: Makeover design, Posh Rooms; pp. 16–19, 20–23: Makeover and project designs, Jane and Greg Peterson; pp. 24–29: Makeover design, Jean Nayar and Margaret Kemp, project designs, Jean Nayar; pp. 30–37, 38–41, 42–45, 46–51, 52–57: Makeover and project designs, Jane and Greg Peterson; pp. 58–61: Makeover and project designs, Jean Nayar; pp. 62–69: Makeover design, Reflections of You; pp. 70–77: Makeover design, Posh Rooms; pp. 78–85, Makeover and project designs, Ingrid Leess; pp. 86–91: Makeover and project designs, Jean Nayar; pp. 92–99: Makeover design, Reflections of You.

PHOTOGRAPHS: p. 1: John Gruen; pp. 2–3: Elizabeth Glasgow; p. 8: John Gruen; pp. 12-15, 16–19: Gridley & Graves; pp. 20–23: Paul Whicheloe; pp. 24–29: Elizabeth Glasgow; pp. 30–37: Aimee Herring; pp. 38–41: Gridley & Graves; pp. 42–45: Paul Whicheloe; pp. 46–51: John Gruen; pp. 52–57: Gridley & Graves; pp. 58–61: Paul Whicheloe; pp. 62–69: Philip Clayton-Thompson; pp. 70–73, 74–77: Gridley & Graves; pp. 78–85: John Gruen; pp. 86–91: Ryan Benyi; pp. 92–99: Philip Clayton-Thompson.
Cover, first flap: Ryan Benyi; back cover (clockwise from top): Elizabeth Glasgow, John Gruen, Gridley & Graves; back flap: John Gruen.

Texts by Mervyn Kaufman and Jean Nayar.
Reporting by Michele Filon.